SALES
RAMP UP

To successful small businesses everywhere!

[signature]

2018

SALES
RAMP UP

How to
KICK  START
PERFORMANCE
AND ADAPT TO CHAOS
with 11-19 Employees

LAURIE L. TAYLOR

Printed in the United States of America.

ISBN: 978-1515340911

This publication is designed to provide accurate and authoritative information in regard to the subject matter covered. It is sold with the understanding that the publisher is not engaged in rendering legal, accounting, or other professional services. If legal advice or other expert assistance is required, the services of a competent professional person should be sought.

TABLE OF CONTENTS

What's Next? 169

INTRODUCTION

You aren't sure when it happened, but without being cognizant of it, you have between 11 – 19 employees. That's a lot of people who rely on you to bring home the bacon. You are now the proud owner of a Stage 2 company!

Stage 2 is all about ramping up for growth –now is the time to start delegating responsibility to capable people and your focus needs to shift to managing the changes that accompany growth.

Have you noticed that things are getting more difficult to manage? It's harder and harder to keep up with the flow of work. Your employees are sending you not so subtle messages that unless you do something soon to ease their pain, it might be you they fry up in a pan.

As you ramp up in Stage 2, focus on driving revenue and increasing profits, getting critical processes in place and avoid the trap of throwing people at your problems. This common mistake alone is responsible for the premature implosion of countless businesses. The additional overhead that more people bring to an organization can quickly overtax a growing company and most Stage 2 leaders feel completely overwhelmed.

Stage 2 is when many business owners suffer burn out. You're not only trying to keep your staff on track with projects, you're still doing everything that starting a business entails. You likely haven't spent much time thinking about managers or even shifting the responsibility of managing additional people to others.

With 11 – 19 employees, you're beginning to see diversification within the organization and the need for infrastructure. People begin to differentiate their tasks and start to become specialists within the organization.

As companies grow, the complexity level of the organization increases. That complexity level doesn't increase because of revenues, profits or equity growth. Complexity increases because of the one factor in a company that is the hardest to control: PEOPLE!

Focus on driving revenue and increasing profits.

James Fischer, author of the 7 Stages of Growth and the book, *Navigating the Growth Curve*, discovered that as companies add more people to the equation, the dynamics change. Fischer developed the 7 Stages of Growth to address entrepreneurial companies struggling to manage growth, from 1 – 500 employees. I worked with him for five years as a managing partner at Origin Institute.

Through my current company, FlashPoint!, I have spoken to thousands of CEOs regarding the unique 7 Stages of Growth business model. The results are overwhelming. The information resonates with CEOs immediately.

At a presentation to over a hundred business owners, a seasoned CEO, now running his twelfth company, said:

> *"After eighteen years of doing turnarounds and twelve years of investment banking, I finally found a system that prescribes the*

ideal management styles and focus for different sized companies. I am on the board of a private company and will be applying the Stages of Growth techniques when advising this company."

This reaction is typical from a CEO who has been around the block, who understands the challenges of growing a successful company and who understands that simply reading the next how-to, book of the month isn't a formula for building a successful company.

The 7 Stages of Growth gets CEO's attention because the concepts allow a business owner to do three things.

1. Predict how growth will impact them.
2. Focus on the right things at the right time.
3. Adapt leadership styles to the changes necessitated by growth.

This model allows you to look at the past, the present and the future in order to better understand what hidden agents are impacting your ability to grow. Once you identify those hidden agents and put a name to the underlying issues, you can solve them and move on.

The 7 Stages of Growth provides every single employee the ability to understand the challenges a company faces as it grows. Each challenge can be talked about in terms everyone understands, thus taking the mystery out of running a company.

The impact of creating a "language of growth" starts with understanding that language doesn't *describe* a person's experience, it *defines* their experience. Change the language and you change the experience.

> *"The Stages of Growth definitely brought clarity to ASBA's toughest challenges. We were aware of the things that had been holding us back, but by going through the process and identifying the challenges, it helped us to prioritize and to focus on the solutions. Sometimes it is easy to get overwhelmed with all the things that 'need' to be done to take an organization to the next level. The 7 Stages of Growth helped us understand our organization much better at a root level, which helped us then determine the best path of success."*
>
> -Rick Murray, CEO, Arizona Small Business Association

In talking with business owners every day, I know they struggle to keep their focus on the constant barrage of issues. A fast-growing enterprise can quickly grow beyond the owner's ability to manage everything.

This book addresses critical areas of focus for a Stage 2 Company. You may not define growth by the addition of employees. You may think growth means creating a business that allows you to have a solid income for as long as you want it. Or, you may just be starting to consider the amazing possibilities your company has to offer and are looking for ways of managing it as you grow.

Because Fischer's model is built on the premise that says as you add people, you add complexity, a business owner has to make it a high priority to build the kind of environment that attracts, focuses and keeps talented employees. To that end, building a profitable company depends upon your ability to manage people.

It's my goal to continue to provide you resources that help you turn your good company into a great company.

If you have read my first book, *Survive and Thrive: How to Unlock Profits in a Startup with 1 – 10 Employees*, you will notice that some of the challenges that impacted a Stage 1 company are also Stage 2 challenges. If you have already addressed those challenges in Stage 1, you can simply ignore them and focus your energy on the new challenges.

The end result is yours to determine. You have taken the first step in developing a strong foundation by considering the research-proven concepts that support the 7 Stages of Growth enterprise development model. If your company continues to add employees, I hope you return to my websites often to learn more about the challenges of each of the 7 Stages of Growth.

I wish you success in growing your business!

Your success. My passion.

Laurie Taylor, President
FlashPoint! LLC
www.bizchallenges.com
www.igniteyourbiz.com
www.destination-greatness.com
www.growthcurvespecialists.com

What a Stage 2 Company Looks Like

A Stage 2 company has 11 – 19 employees. At this juncture, it's all about ramping up sales and managing growth. Your top challenge is hiring quality people. As the CEO of a Stage 2 company, you're still the center of the business. Keep your wits about you and before you react to the increase in activity and workload, ask yourself these questions:

- Am I still focused on driving profits and revenue?
- Am I beginning to let go of critical aspects of the company to capable people?
- Am I monitoring the key indicators of success every day?

In Stage 1, everyone wore all the hats and could do everything. The ability of everyone in the company to be generalists fueled the growth and created a culture that was fun to be a part of. As a Stage

2 leader, you start seeing the beginning of diversification within the organizational infrastructure.

Now the real challenges of growing a sustainable business come into play; it's no longer just about survival. You have to differentiate the jobs and tasks that need to be done and start to develop specialists. Get very clear on roles and responsibilities. This isn't as easy as it sounds, but being aggressive now will save you a lot of stumbling when you move into Stage 3.

This is a critical stage in that you must begin to delegate both authority and responsibility, which is difficult for many entrepreneurs. There is a strong tendency to want to hold on to all of the control and continue to make all of the decisions. The reality is you simply can't.

Many Stage 2 leaders feel they are stretched too thin and grow frustrated that people aren't doing their jobs. There is a very real fear that things are getting out of control.

One of the biggest barriers to delegation is the false perception that you don't have enough time to adequately explain the tasks or to teach your team the skills necessary. The tendency is to try to continue doing everything yourself. Even though you may be faster and know more today, this practice is not sustainable. Your span of control (the number of people one person can effectively manage) has increased beyond your ability to manage the increasing size of your organization. One of the main benefits of delegation is to save time.

As a company navigates through Stage 2, one primary goal is to determine if the business model you started with as a Stage 1 organization is still viable. A CEO should evaluate how the company will grow and think about:

1. Value Proposition
2. Customers/Channel
3. Product/Service Features/Benefits
4. Revenue Model
5. Marketing and Sales Processes
6. Operations Process
7. Profitability
8. Cash Flow

A Stage 2 company is still CEO-centric. The functions of the organization still rely on the CEO's vision, energy, passion and knowledge of products, services and customers.

The CEO also still needs to manage sales. The sales process should be defined at this stage so it can be replicated. Customers tend to grow dependent on working directly with the business owner, particularly in small, growing operations. Creating a process that allows a new sales person to seamlessly manage product or service development is important as you grow. A business owner who continues to drive sales and manage all of the workload is vulnerable for burnout. Energy must be focused on growing the organization by handing off aspects of running the company to others. This process begins with surrounding yourself with capable people.

As the CEO of a Stage 2 company, 40% of your time should be spent fine-tuning the vision of the company, while another 40% should be spent as the technician or the specialist. As you ramp up for growth, 20% of your time should be devoted to managing people, a responsibility that will continue to increase as you grow. This percentage blend is referred to as the Three Faces of a Leader. We'll talk about this concept in greater detail a little later on.

> A business owner who continues to drive sales and manage all of the workload is vulnerable for burnout.

Now is the time to examine your leadership strengths and weaknesses. Your ability to make people feel a part of something special is vital during this stage.

Myron Rogers, in Margaret Wheatley's book, *Finding Our Way*, challenges us to think of our organizations as adaptive, flexible, self-renewing, resilient, learning and intelligent: the same attributes found in living systems. And according to Rogers, "you can never direct a living system, you can only disturb it."

Encourage the people within your organization to respond intentionally to continual change. The process of building something that moves beyond any one person's ability creates a cohesive team that will be well poised for growth.

Rogers identified three questions to ask your team:

1. Why are we doing this?
2. What's possible now that we've agreed to try this together?
3. How does the purpose of this effort connect to my personal sense of purpose and to the purposes of the larger system?

By growing your company, you are challenging your people to grow. When you start this process early, you are able to tap into the intelligence of every single person.

A Stage 2 company must also focus on cost issues to support a higher sales level and generate positive cash flow as well as profits. Growth, not survival, is the driver.

REQUIRED LEADERSHIP SKILL BASE

- Effective sales management
- Strong, responsive customer service product/service quality controls
- Cost controls in place on key indicators
- Manage growth and wear most of the hats
- The ability to sell your vision to a small loyal staff that can move mountains
- The willingness to fix and tinker with critical processes
- Continuously improving hiring processes

You are still the center of the business and all decisions run past you. Constant vigilance is required. In the scurry of rapid growth, it's easy to overlook key indicators, cash flow can become thin and disaster is right around the corner.

My promise to Stage 2 leaders – those of you running companies with 11 – 19 employees, is this:

If you embrace the 5 Challenges that I'm going to outline and take the time to study them and apply the knowledge I'll share with you,

> Growth, not survival, is the driver.

you will start to build a foundation for your company that will serve you well; whether you stay in Stage 2 or grow your business up to a Stage 7, with 161 – 500 employees.

How do I know that? Because as the owner and partner of a multi-million dollar company that I helped grow from two to over 100 employees, we struggled in Stage 2 for all the reasons I'm going to cover with you in here. And because we struggled, we lost critical traction and when you lose traction, you create even more chaos. We grew to over $12 million in sales. However, we would have grown to over $50 million in sales if I had known then what I know now.

PREDICTING GROWTH

As I present the 7 Stages of Growth to CEOs all around the country, I know two things.

1. If you are starting or running a company, you are smart, energetic, capable, able to think outside the box, willing to put in long hours, have a strong vision, believe 150% in your product or service and feel overwhelmed most of the time.

2. You'd like a structure that you can utilize to help you figure out what is coming, how to manage the hundreds of issues that you deal with every day and

how to make sure you survive to the next stage of your business's growth cycle.

> If you continue your journey with me, I guarantee I can help you accomplish three things.
>
> 1. Figure out why you are struggling to stay focused.
> 2. Show you that you can predict how growth will impact you.
> 3. Help you understand what you need to do to adapt to the changes your company is going through.

In the early stages of growing a company, you need to ask core questions such as:

- How do I plan on targeting, capturing and caring for my customers?
- Am I tracking my revenue by revenue groups in order to understand where I generate the best margins?
- Are we horizontally or vertically integrated?
- What is our dominant culture?
- How will we capture and encourage knowledge?
- What is the relationship our company has with the customer, our vendors, our allies and our competitors?

This book is designed to help a Stage 2 CEO understand where to focus her energies in order to get the most traction as she starts to build a successful company.

When James Fischer interviewed growth-smart companies in his 7 Stages of Growth research study, he was able to identify 27 specific challenges that business owners experienced as they grew. Business owners find value in these 27 challenges because they finally have a starting point to talk about what's going on in their business.

In Stage 2 companies, he recognized that successful CEOs had figured out how to hire quality people. They knew the importance of keeping those key employees aware of where the company was going and how their position, what they did every day, would help the company succeed.

He was able to create a language of growth and turn those successes into areas that CEOs needed to pay attention to. Fischer referred to these as the "stages of growth challenges." His premise was that CEOs should focus on these critical challenges at each stage of growth in order to minimize the chaos that can create obstacles to growth.

It's hard for business owners, bombarded by issues every day, to articulate what is going on for them. They know something is creating a problem, but they can't identify what it is. The 27 Challenges define in a few words what business owners are experiencing. That's a big step when you are trying to engage a team of people to help you fix something. The value of understanding the stages of growth is that throughout the model, we are guiding the CEO on how to prioritize their time, energy and dollars.

As this book suggests, there are 5 top challenges a Stage 2 leader should focus on. As your company grows, you will eventually have to tackle all 27.

THE 27 CHALLENGES

1. Profits are inadequate to grow the company
2. Need for an improved profit design
3. Customers are migrating away from products/ services
4. Continual cash flow challenges
5. Limited capital available to grow
6. Employee turnover
7. Hiring quality staff
8. Staff morale and voltage challenges
9. Need for a flexible planning model
10. Need to have better staff buy-in
11. Project management and resource coordination challenges
12. Leadership/staff communication gap
13. New staff orientation
14. Staff training
15. Unclear values throughout the organization
16. Dealing with the cost of lost expertise or knowledge when employees leave
17. Chaotic periods destabilize company
18. Organization needs to understand how the company will grow in the future, not just the leadership
19. Organization needs to better understand the impact that staff satisfaction has on the company's profitability
20. Company culture is generally resistant to change
21. The marketplace and your customers change too quickly

22. Difficulty forecasting problem areas before they surface
23. Difficulty diagnosing the real problems or obstacles to growth
24. Too slow getting new products/services to market
25. Not able to quickly get systems and procedures in place as the company is growing
26. Weak product/service development and differentiation in market
27. Expanding sales

THE TOP 5 CHALLENGES OF A STAGE 2 COMPANY

The ability to help a CEO get clear about the right things at the right time is what separates high performing companies from mediocre companies. The small percentage of companies that succeed are the ones that tend to stay ahead of their growth curve.

The Top 5 Challenges for a Stage 2 Company, in this order, are:

1. **Hiring quality people**

2. **Expanding sales**

3. **Continual cash flow challenges**

4. **Leadership/Staff communication gap**

5. **Limited capital to grow**

Key Growth Concepts

You now know what a Stage 2 company looks like and that I am committed to helping business owners predict growth's impact.

Now, it is important to cover three other elements that are part of the Stages of Growth language. They are the 4 Rules that govern the 7 Stages of Growth, understanding the Transition Zones between stages and the Three Gates of Focus.

THE 4 RULES THAT GOVERN THE 7 STAGES OF GROWTH

As a business owner navigates their own growth curve, there are 4 critical rules that serve as guideposts to walk the fine line between chaos and equilibrium.

RULE #1:
THE MOVEMENT FROM ONE STAGE OF GROWTH TO ANOTHER BEGINS AS SOON AS YOU LAND IN ANY STAGE OF GROWTH.

You don't simply become a Stage 2 company overnight. The process starts as soon as you enter Stage 1.

> Think of the Stages of Growth as a continuum that moves ahead based on your strategic plan.

If you plan to grow to 18 employees in the next 18 months, now is the time to plan! This is what sets the 7 Stages of Growth apart from other models. A CEO can actually *predict* when they will move into a new stage of growth and be able to adjust *before* they arrive.

RULE #2:
WHAT YOU DON'T GET DONE IN A SPECIFIC STAGE OF GROWTH DOES NOT GO AWAY.

The challenges for your current stage of growth need to be addressed before you move into a new stage. There are many cases in which you can blow through a stage of growth very quickly, by acquiring outside funding or another company, which adds to the headcount. If one of these scenarios presents itself, be sure to remain alert to the needs of your current stage of growth.

Focus on the specific People, Process and Profit/Revenue challenges in your current stage of growth today so that you are well prepared for tomorrow. Remember, the complexity of an organization will always extract its due. Don't be lulled into a false sense of security; there is always a price to pay for rapid growth.

RULE #3:
TIME WILL MAKE A DIFFERENCE.

Time is an important factor because slower growth is easier to manage. If you're a Stage 2 company with 18 employees and you have been that way for 15 years, you've grown slowly and addressed your challenges as you grew.

However, if you blew through Stage 1 overnight, there is strong chance that the issues you should have addressed early on are still unresolved. The time rule is a reminder to pay attention to the challenges that are specific to each growth stage.

> *"About half of all new establishments survive five years or more and about one third survive 10 years or more. As one would expect, the probability of survival increases with a firm's age. Survival rates have changed little over time."*
> - Source: U.S. Bureau of Labor Statistics

If your company has been in the same stage of growth for five years or longer, look at the specific challenges that lie ahead to proactively manage growth. Check in with your company to ensure that your current stage of growth's challenges have been addressed in depth. Business leaders have a tendency to focus on surface issues without looking under the hood. Address stage specific challenges at the time, so they don't rear their ugly heads later, because they will.

Many companies intentionally stay a certain size but grow in other dimensions, especially in Stages 1 and 2. Even if your business model caps the number of employees you have, heed the challenges for your stage to grow stronger and more profitable.

RULE #4:
IF YOU AREN'T GROWING, YOU'RE DYING.

In order to stay fresh and current, something in your organization has to grow and change. The concept behind the stages of growth is similar to growth in nature, which has its own mechanisms to stir the pot. A static condition in nature or in business is indicative of imminent death.

We are all familiar with the process that a caterpillar goes through to turn into a butterfly, often described as one of the most intriguing transformations in the animal kingdom. If something goes wrong during the chrysalis stage, the butterfly won't emerge from the cocoon. Same with a company; if the wheels come off the business in the early stages of growth, it may never recover.

As human beings, we have a tendency to gravitate toward a state of equilibrium because it is safe and understandable. If we stay in that state too long, it actually causes a slow dying away, just as in nature. Getting ahead of your growth curve allows you to recognize the signs of change and gives you time to react.

So, the answer to the question, "Do We Need to Grow?" is categorically YES. Even in a downturn economy when revenues are shrinking and profits melting away, there are areas of improvement a company can focus on. The challenge for business owners in any stage of growth is to make sure they define growth for the company and not let growth define them.

TAKING THE TIME TO GET IT RIGHT

Ron Grob is an extraordinary company because of its rich history and its plans for the future. Knowledge of both is essential to understanding the company. Since its inception, Ron Grob built its reputation as a job shop that excelled in thread rolling and centerless grinding. In the early 1990s, the company expanded its capabilities to include CNC Swiss screw machining and CNC vertical machining. As the shop continued to expand, it quickly earned a positive reputation in Colorado's Front Range as a one-stop shop. The Ron Grob Company became the premier manufacturer of complex parts that other shops have trouble producing consistently well.

Part of the Ron Grob strategy was to diversify the customer base, both in industries served and in number of customers. According to Harold Huffaker, VP of Operations and General Manager, "Today, we have jobs from 50 different customers on the shop floor on any given day and this includes customers large and small. We build parts for companies in the medical, water management, firearms, military, as well as the gas and oil industries." The Ron Grob Company has found that these particular industries benefit greatly from the services they provide.

Harold and the owner of the company, Ron Grob, heard me give a presentation on the 7 Stages of Growth in March of 2009. It was soon after that connection that I started to work with Harold and his team. Harold and Ron saw themselves in the model. They felt the challenges they were experiencing lined up exactly with the definition of a Stage 1 company, with 1 – 10 employees.

The Rob Grob Company had maintained its status in Stage 2, with between 11 – 19 employees, for several years. The decision to remain at that size was deliberate. The company endured many tense moments during the recession. By staying close to their core customers and continuing to deliver high-quality products, the company made it through those tough times and learned some key lessons.

Growing didn't have to mean getting bigger. It meant being able to manage the expectations of their employees and customers to avoid over-promising and under delivering. It required a management team that was in sync with the upward direction the business was heading, but also aware of the challenges of growing with intention. Passion is a necessary ingredient to being on the management team at the Ron Grob Company. They are collectively juggling daily operations and fostering a profit, all while simultaneously driving the business to the next level of precision machining.

Today, they have just breached Stage 3 and have 20 employees.

The team is working together to better define processes, improve communications and getting ready for the challenges that a Stage 3 company will face. By intentionally focusing on the challenges of a Stage 2 company, Harold and his team are cautiously optimistic about their next stage of growth.

Harold says, "I continue to utilize Laurie Taylor at FlashPoint! as my business coach and I have extended her reach to coaching the entire management team at Ron Grob."

Excerpts from this story are taken from an article that appeared in A2Z Metalworker magazine, Rocky Mountain edition, Sept/Oct 2014.

CRITICAL TRANSITION ZONES

THE FLOOD ZONE

Between each stage of growth lies a transition zone, which is a phase of chaos that the organization moves through in preparation for the next stage of growth. These transition zones are an important juncture in the growth model of any growth organization.

The transition zone between Stage 1 and Stage 2 is called the Flood Zone, named as such because the level of activity increases to the point where people can feel like they are drowning. There are more employees, more clients and more processes that need to be followed. The CEO's tendency is to add more people, but that only intensifies the problems.

This flood of activity will impact your small and growing team the hardest, especially if you haven't taken the time to upgrade your technology or improve your processes. A smooth transition requires an intentional plan to stay in touch with your employees and to effectively manage sales and cash.

> The level of activity increases to the point where people can feel like they are drowning.

A Flood Zone forces leadership to find new ways of dealing with the increased workload. Examine your processes and training programs, explore systems that track customer information and begin to think about what positions you will need to hire when the time is right.

Here's an example of a Flood Zone in action. Let's look at a small manufacturing company in Pennsylvania that's been in business for 30 years. A growth spurt took them from Stage 1 to Stage 2. It's a stable, well-run company with a strong and capable president and loyal employees.

An increase in customer accounts caused invoices and calls to suppliers to grow by 30%. The CEO's wakeup call came when the company was suddenly behind on invoicing by two weeks. She knew revenues were growing but underestimated the impact the new growth would have on standard existing activities such as invoicing. The Flood Zone she encountered wasn't something she could control, but she and her employees would have been better prepared for it if she were able to identify the subtle changes that growth created.

During a Flood Zone, there is an increased level of confusion. Change occurs daily and employees start looking for someone to blame, usually through mumbled curses directed at leadership for putting the company in "this mess."

A good offense is better than a solid defense. Take the time to explain to your staff what's going on as the company transitions through this period. Don't assume they are okay. Just because you understand the reality of growing a business, doesn't mean your employees do. Be aware that your employees are the ones who experience this increase in activity right away. They don't always know their limitations and are likely afraid to admit they are having issues.

This zone helps to create a language of growth, which allows employees to put a name to their pain and derive a measure of comfort. Utilize the language of growth to prepare employees for the chaos that comes with change.

THE WIND TUNNEL

The transition zone into Stage 3 (20 – 34 employees) is called the Wind Tunnel and requires you to let go of old methodologies that no longer work and embrace new ones that do. You can read more about this transition zone in my third book, *The Art of Delegation: How to Effectively Let Go with 20 – 34 Employees.*

THE THREE GATES OF FOCUS

PROFIT/REVENUE, PEOPLE AND PROCESS

There are three gates of focus that a CEO can use to clarify the root cause of an issue. If a CEO can identify the root cause, and help employees do the same, issues can get resolved sooner. Every issue you face in your organization can be categorized under one of these gates. The Three Gates (Profit/Revenue, People and Process) are always stacked in order of importance for that particular stage of growth. For Stage 2, the top gate of focus is Profit/Revenue.

◇◇

The **Profit/Revenue Gate** means that a company is predicting growth by maximizing and anticipating profit/revenue protection and capacity issues.

Sales capacity

Marketing capacity

Facilities capacity

Fulfillment capacity

Capital availability

Production capacity

Product development capacity

The **People Gate** focuses on building competency, staff satisfaction, performance and innovation through the conscious development of people.

Hiring and training

Competitive benefits

On-going and consistent training

Employee engagement

Vision, mission and core values

Performance indicators

Empowerment support

Management training

Leadership development

The **Process Gate** means transforming complexity into clarity through processes.

Strategy/planning processes

Forecasting/tracking processes

Knowledge management processes

Customer intelligence processes

Operational processes

Project management processes

Human resource processes

Work community processes

◇◇◇

Let's look at an example of a Stage 2 CEO, Lisa, who has just been told by Mike, one of her employees that he is struggling with a project. Often, the tendency is to lay blame on individuals instead of digging deeper to see if the problem is a process issue or even a profit (can we afford it?) issue.

To better understand the problem, Lisa asked Mike, "Do you think the issue is People, Profit or Process related? This specific question forces Mike to think more seriously about the underlying issue and not just focus on what is showing up on the surface. Given the language, he may say that it's a People Issue and he needs more training; or he may identify that it's a Process Issue because the system they are using is no longer effective; or he may identify it as a Profit Issue, explaining that a critical piece of equipment is broken and needs to be replaced. This brief but impactful conversation helps Lisa adopt a problem-solving approach and gives Mike a new way to approach the problem.

Language is the world's greatest change agent. Successful business owners instinctively know that you seed change in an enterprise by shifting and transforming the baseline language of the workplace community. People converse and communicate within the boundaries of the current language that describes their experience. Language doesn't just *describe* an experience; it *defines* it. Change the language and you change the experience.

For whatever reason, the financials of many businesses remain clouded in a language that confuses, rather than clarifies. Most people would prefer to leave this aspect up to the numbers people and be in the dark. Trying to explain a balance sheet to your employees is a little like trying to explain how an internal combustion engine works to someone who is not at all mechanically inclined. If, however, you explain the drive mechanisms (spark plug, gasoline, piston, camshaft, transmission) that start the car moving forward, it all starts to make sense.

Adopt a similar approach when explaining to your employees that there are three ways to increase how much money you make: volume, price and cost. You can increase the volume of what you sell, you can increase the sale price or decrease the production cost. Once your employees understand how they directly impact these three factors, lights go on!

> Language doesn't just **describe** an experience; it **defines** it.

Suddenly, the financials are something they not only understand, but something they can talk about. The language shifts from the dry "earnings ratio to net profit" to a more engaged and educated interpretation: "We increased our price by 15%, increased our volume by 5%, decreased our costs by 20% and brought in an additional $50,000 in our first quarter." This is a powerful way to engage the entire company in understanding the financial impacts within your business.

One of the core values of the 7 Stages of Growth model is in its ability to help a company focus on the right things at the right time. The Gates of Focus allow everyone the opportunity to clarify issues quickly and reduce the chaos that comes with misdiagnosing a problem. In addition to providing clarity, the Three Gates of Focus begins the process of creating a language of growth. Throughout the 7 Stages, there are many opportunities for a CEO to help every employee understand what is going in the company's growth cycle.

THREE GATES OF FOCUS FOR STAGE 1 AND STAGE 2

STAGE 1 (1 - 10 EMPLOYEES)	STAGE 2 (11-19 EMPLOYEES)
Profit/Revenue Gate	Profit/Revenue Gate
People Gate	Process Gate
Process Gate	People Gate

As in Stage 1, the top gate of focus for Stage 2 is still Profit/ Revenue. However in Stage 1, the second gate of focus was People followed by Process. Process was the last gate of focus because with fewer people, you can still manage workload with fewer processes.

In Stage 2, the priorities shift slightly; Profit/Revenue is followed by Process and then People. The Process Gate becomes more critical because with up to 19 employees, you have to start thinking about how to create efficiencies to manage the workload better and protect profit. This subtle shift, creating processes that ensure efficient and effective workflow, is the single most important change a leader can make to ensure profitability.

Hidden Agents

WHAT IS A HIDDEN AGENT?

Hidden agents provide CEOs with a language to identify critical issues that may be creating obstacles to their growth. By understanding a company's hidden agents, a CEO can get to the root cause of a problem faster and engage their management team to help identify the right issues.

HIDDEN AGENT #1: BUILDER/PROTECTOR RATIO

More than likely, if you own a business, you understand a Builder mentality. You create new ideas, take on new initiatives and find ways to expand the revenue and profitability of your company. You choose to challenge and improve the way things are done, thrive on risk and are highly supportive of growth.

A Protector mindset is cautious and prefers to slow down the pace of change. They are risk averse and highly suspicious of growth. Protectors may not feel confident in the company's financial strength and are slow to embrace the optimism of the future.

Builder/Protector measures the intensity and the balance between the state of confidence and the state of caution inherent in the psyche of an organization. This measurement allows a CEO and their leadership team to assess the company's ability to accept change and successfully navigate the change. React with confidence to that change and you help the company achieve its stated goals.

A company's Builder/Protector Ratio will change based on its current stage of growth. This hidden agent is expressed as a ratio such as 3 Builders to 1 Protector (3:1), which is the optimal Builder/Protector Ratio during Stage 2.

BUILDERS:

- Create new ideas
- Take on new initiatives
- Find ways to expand the revenue and profits
- Challenge the way things are done
- Are risk tolerant and highly supportive of growth
- Are highly confident
- Are always looking for new opportunities
- Don't back down from everyday challenges

PROTECTORS:

- Are cautious and slow paced
- Are risk averse
- May not feel confident in the company's financial strength
- Tend to be suspicious of new markets
- Prefer to apply the brakes (and should be encouraged to do so when appropriate)

Too much Protector, the company could stall. Too much Builder, the company could fail. Moving too slow or moving too fast will make management more difficult and the top executive will continually struggle to gain buy-in.

The CEO must not only be a Builder, she must develop a team that, for the most part, is like-minded in order to persevere through the challenges of a startup. But, a bit of the Protector mindset is helpful to counter the Builder's tendency to be eternal optimists with tunnel vision.

DETERMINING YOUR COMPANY'S BUILDER/PROTECTOR RATIO

There are specific signs that will immediately let you know how balanced your Builder/Protector Ratio is. A leader can get a good idea of their company's B/P Ratio by:

1. Tuning into the voltage (think energy) in the company
2. Talking to the leadership team and asking some pointed questions
3. Really listening to your employees

What are the signs? Are people engaged in open and active dialogue? Are meetings productive and full of valuable information? Are good decisions being made?

What are the questions? Does your leadership team or your employees appear optimistic about the future? Are they confident in the financial strength of the company? Do they have a high level of confidence in their co-workers?

What are your employees saying? Is there a lot of behind the scenes gossiping? Is there a high rate of absenteeism or turnover? Do your managers or employees complain about a lack of accountability? Are projects derailed or slowed down too often?

You can move between this Builder/Protector mindset as the circumstances or situations require. You need to continually balance your confidence with a certain amount of caution, as the team will take its cues from how you respond to challenges. If the company expands too fast and cash flow becomes tight, you need to be the voice of caution that pulls back and rethinks that next hire or decision to expand your operation. However, staying too long in the Protector mindset isn't healthy for the organization. Simply recognizing when and how this hidden agent is impacting your company is why the Builder/Protector Ratio is an important indicator for growth.

WHAT IS TOO MUCH WHEN IT COMES TO THE BUILDER/PROTECTOR MINDSET?

While the results of a Builder mindset tend to manifest in ways that help a company grow (drive sales, look for new opportunities, strong financials), too much Builder mindset can create issues, just as a Protector mindset can restrict growth if applied too often or for prolonged periods of time.

SYMPTOMS OF TOO MUCH BUILDER:

1) Hockey stick sales projections

2) Hiring in advance of need

3) Taking on higher risk projects without proper reward

4) Over-committing and under-delivering

5) Lack of clarity in the direction of the company

SYMPTOMS OF TOO MUCH PROTECTOR:

1) Unwilling to try new marketing and business development techniques

2) Too much focus on expenses, not enough on revenue

3) See hurdles instead of opportunities

4) Insulated, not seeking divergent opinions

5) Leaders seem fearful about the future and stop communicating

6) The business is hesitant to embrace change

7) Decisions take too long and opportunities are missed

Continually balance your confidence with a certain amount of caution.

Understanding your company's Builder/Protector Ratio improves your insight into your company's mental health by:

1. Allowing you to measure the company's ability to meet and overcome challenges.
2. Communicating the company's willingness to perceive and take advantage of opportunities in its path.
3. Measuring the strength of the company's immune defense system, acting as a barrier against low morale and poor performance.
4. Assessing the company's willingness to advance itself through change.
5. Telegraphing the company's belief in its future.
6. Communicating the company's trust in its leaders.

WHEN THE BUILDER/PROTECTOR RATIO IS OUT OF ALIGNMENT

The Builder/Protector Ratio is a powerful concept and once a CEO and her team understands it, the dynamics in a management team, and ultimately a company, can change within weeks.

Let me give you an example. The owner of a manufacturing company has 17 employees. After growing to this size in just 4 years, this owner is experiencing headaches typical for a company in this stage of growth.

ISSUES INCLUDE:

1. The inability of the CEO to release control to key employees — creating a sense of distrust among every single person in the company.

2. No defined values that help drive the behaviors of each person in the company, promoting a lackadaisical attitude among the more experienced employees because they don't see bad behavior dealt with.

3. Questions about growth go unanswered more than likely because the CEO hasn't created a vision for the company or felt the need to share it with people if it does exist.

4. Decision making is only done at the CEO level because employees know that their decisions will be belittled, not just questioned, leaving employees thinking that not asking is better than taking a risk in asking.

5. Experienced employees want to step up and take a more active role in running the company but receive no encouragement. They lose the motivation to pursue their own professional growth because of perceived lack of trust and willingness on the part of the CEO to let go of authority and responsibility.

6. Communication does not exist between the CEO and key staff members. The CEO is involved in production day in and day out, there are no regular staff meetings to share information and staff members are left wondering what is expected and even more importantly what they are supposed to be doing.

7. The CEO firmly believes that people just need to step up and do their jobs. She shows impatience, and in fact, considers it a weakness when people can't make decisions, ask too many questions and appear to not understand what is expected of them.

This is a company headed for disaster. Will it happen right away? No. And many companies continue to expand and grow with the issues outlined above. Whenever there are employees, there is an expectation that the CEO is there to guide, direct, manage, coach and discipline the staff.

In James Fischer's book, *Navigating the Growth Curve*, he introduces a unique phenomenon that indicated there is a blend of confidence and caution in every company. Successful CEOs understood this ratio and that it was their responsibility to provide balance to move their companies forward.

The CEO of that small manufacturing company referenced earlier is unknowingly creating a company of Protectors through her need to control and her hesitation to bring her employees into the vision and strategic plans for the company.

Her controlling nature has virtually shut down the Builder-like capability in every single employee. By discouraging communication, the Builders will not step up or take risks and will quickly revert to Protector status. This tendency is reinforced when a CEO doesn't share information about the company's future plans or the current financial picture.

A company that had huge potential for growth can suddenly find itself with a culture of resistance, high turnover and a very frustrated CEO.

When the Builder/Protector Ratio is out of alignment, a CEO can send a signal to her team that she is not confident about the direction of the company without even being aware of it. That lack of confidence will manifest in key employees or the management team, and ultimately ricochet throughout the entire company.

A Stage 2 company is still CEO-centric, so if the CEO is overly cautious, she could unwittingly bring the company to a grinding halt. Confidence is critical in any stage of growth. In the early stages of a company expanding its sales and customer base, if the Builder/ Protector Ratio is less than 3:1, the company may lose traction.

IF A COMPANY IS AWARE OF ITS B/P RATIO IT CAN:

1. Make good decisions in a timely manner
2. Accept change as a part of the company's culture and
3. Engage employees in meaningful dialogue because they have helped design the strategic future of the company.

Remember, a confident company is a profitable company.

THE BUILDER/PROTECTOR RATIO FOR STAGE 1 AND STAGE 2

STAGE 1 (1-10 EMPLOYEES)	STAGE 2 (11-19 EMPLOYEES)
4:1	3:1

HIDDEN AGENT #2: THREE FACES OF A LEADER

The 7 Stages of Growth research uncovered the Three Faces of a Leader. The length of time a leader spends wearing one of these faces depends upon their stage of growth. There is a model percentage blend for each stage.

For a Stage 2 company, the Three Faces blend looks like this:

VISIONARY: 40%

Visionary leaders ensure the company knows where it wants to go. They can take the most insignificant situation and turn it into an opportunity. It's important that leaders in Stage 2 continue to share the vision and continually check in with their growing number of employees to help keep that vision alive. As with Stage 1, there is still a lot of chaos and uncertainty with a Stage 2 company. In the chaos of growth, employees can lose sight of the bigger picture and question why they are doing what they are doing.

Spend time talking with your employees about how they see the company and find out what they think the company's strengths and weaknesses are. Help them to see themselves in the future of the organization and challenge them to continually grow and learn in order to help the company do the same.

MANAGER: 20%

The manager face understands the importance of growing a company through the management of workflow and people. A manager creates order and focuses on pragmatic systems and procedures that make the company run well. This requires emotional intelligence and dedication to helping people succeed.

The manager face has increased from 10% in Stage 1 to 20% in Stage 2. There are more people and they are becoming specialized, which requires more direction. The CEO needs to start "letting it go to let it grow" by releasing authority and responsibility and managing expectations.

For many entrepreneurs, management is difficult to embrace, but the need for strong management grows with the company. This issue will only become more important with additional staff, so devote time to it now.

SPECIALIST: 40%

The specialist face immerses in the work the company produces. They understand the need to capture the necessary processes, to deliver the work and meet clients' needs. In most cases, the specialist is the person who came up with the idea to start the company; she is action oriented and detail focused.

If you have taken a strong role in developing your product or service, now is the time to help your employees step up and play a more active part in delivering that product or service to customers. At this stage, you start to hire for skill and your employees can be expected to provide expertise where necessary. You don't have to have *all* of the answers anymore!

THREE FACES OF A LEADER FOR STAGE 1 AND STAGE 2

STAGE 1 (1-10 EMPLOYEES)	
VISONARY	40%
MANAGER	10%
SPECIALIST	50%

STAGE 2 (11-19 EMPLOYEES)	
VISONARY	40%
MANAGER	20%
SPECIALIST	40%

WHEN THE THREE FACES OF A LEADER BLEND IS OUT OF ALIGNMENT

A CEO of a growing company needs to bring all three faces to the table every day. They provide focus while working to transition the company from a CEO-centric mindset to an Enterprise-centric mindset, which occurs when the company grows from Stage 2 to Stage 3. Essentially, the CEO needs to delegate certain functions, set expectations and follow through to ensure those expectations are being implemented.

Imagine if the CEO spent too much time being a Visionary and not enough time being the Specialist. Taking your eye off the product or service in Stage 2 could impact the future sustainability of that product or service. Remember, as the CEO, it's your passion and energy that helps your employees stay focused and you still play a critical role in fine-tuning the deliverable.

In Stage 2, the CEO spends equal time in the Visionary (40%) and Specialist (40%) roles. With up to 19 employees, the CEO needs to paint the picture of the future so the team clearly sees the part they will play in it. At no other time in a company's life cycle will the CEO have greater influence over the direction, the values and the vision of her company. Focus on driving profit and revenue to protect cash so you can invest in the processes and people you need. Understanding and balancing the three faces of a leader isn't an option for a CEO in Stage 2 – it's an absolute necessity.

> At no other time in a company's life cycle will the CEO have greater influence over the direction, the values and the vision of her company.

HIDDEN AGENT #3: LEADERSHIP STYLE

Leaders create resonance in an organization by ensuring that the entire fabric of a company is laced with emotional intelligence. Developing a new leadership style means changing how one operates with other people.

What do winning leaders have in common?

- They are aware of their own emotions and empathetic toward the people they lead.
- They understand that handling relationships well begins with authenticity: acting from one's genuine feelings.

If a leader behaves disingenuously or manipulatively, for instance, their employees will immediately sense falseness, which leads to distrust. The ability to connect emotionally to the people you lead is important to create an environment that fosters involvement and commitment from everyone in your company.

Your **Leadership Style** communicates mountains of information to everyone in your company.

STYLES NEED TO BE PRACTICED

Leadership is a skill like any other. Anyone who has the will and the motivation can become a better leader. Understanding the steps and taking the time to practice turns a mediocre leader into one who can inspire greatness. Improvement starts with understanding where you are today and what you aspire to be. That's why a solid diagnosis of your leadership strengths and weaknesses and a plan for development are crucial. Tuned-out, dissonant leaders are one of the main reasons that talented people leave a company, taking precious knowledge with them.

Our guiding values are represented in the prefrontal areas of the brain as a hierarchy with what we love at the top and what we loathe at the bottom. What keeps us moving toward our goals comes down to the mind's ability to remind us how satisfied we will feel when we accomplish them.

What does this mean for you as a leader? Wherever people gravitate within their work role indicates where their real pleasure lies and that pleasure is itself motivating. External motivations cannot get people to perform at their absolute best – it's an inside job!

Why do you care? By tuning into the desires, dreams and career goals of your employees, you gain insight into what motivates them. If you can take their passion and turn it into a driving force in their jobs, you've started to build a company that can truly go from being good to great.

KEY LEADERSHIP STYLES

Here is a summary of the six Leadership Styles from Daniel Goleman's book, *Primal Leadership*.

1. **Visionary:** Visionary leaders frame the collective task in terms of a grander vision. Employees are encouraged to innovate and work toward shared goals that build team commitment. People are proud to belong to the organization.

2. **Coaching:** Coaching leaders communicate a belief in people's potentials and an expectation they can do their best. By linking people's daily work to long-term goals, coaches keep people motivated.

3. **Affiliative:** Affiliative leaders recognize employees as people and put less emphasis on accomplishing tasks and goals. Such leaders build tremendous loyalty and strengthen connectedness.

4. **Democratic:** A democratic leader builds on a triad of primal leadership abilities: teamwork and collaboration, conflict management and influence. Listening is the key strength of this "team member" leadership style.

5. **Pacesetting:** A pacesetter leader holds and exemplifies high standards for performance. The foundation of this style lies in the drive to achieve

by continually finding ways to improve their own performance and that of those they lead.

6. **Commanding:** Commanding leaders draw on three primal leadership competencies: influence, achievement and initiative. They exert forceful direction to get better results and opportunities are seized in an unhesitating tone.

Great leaders move us. They ignite our passion and inspire the best in us. When people try to explain great leadership they talk about vision, strategy and powerful ideas. But the reality is great leadership works through emotions. It's *how* you connect to people that successfully gets something done.

Your job as a leader just got harder or easier, depending on how you want to look at it. You have the power to sway everyone's emotions. If you push your people toward enthusiasm, performance will soar. If you drive them toward rancor and anxiety, they will get thrown off stride.

The reason a leader's manner – not just *what* she does but *how* she does it – matters so much lies in the design of the human brain: what scientists have started to call the "open loop" of our emotional centers. A closed loop system, such as the circulatory system, is self-regulating; what's happening in the circulatory system of those around us does not impact our own system. An open loop system depends largely on external sources to manage itself.

> Great leadership works through emotions.

In other words, we rely on connections with other people for our own emotional stability. In intensive care units, research has shown that the comforting presence of another person not only lowers the patient's blood pressure, but also slows the secretion of fatty acids that block arteries.

Here's a startling statistic: three or more incidents of intense stress within a year (financial trouble, job loss or divorce) triple the death rate in socially isolated middle aged men. Alternatively, incidents of stress have zero impact on the death rate of men who cultivate close relationships.

This open loop system says "people need people." The ability of a leader to connect to their people at work can have the same healthy results when that emotional awareness is taken home.

ARE YOU WILLING TO ADJUST YOUR LEADERSHIP STYLE FOR THE GROWTH OF YOUR BUSINESS?

To succeed, leadership development must be the strategic priority of the enterprise. Understanding the six leadership styles and how they impact each stage of growth is a powerful tool for any CEO. In the 7 Stages of Growth enterprise development model, there are three critical leadership styles for each stage of growth and they are stacked in order of importance. All three bring different dynamics to a CEO's management world and the more a CEO understands when to apply each style, the more effective she will be.

For a Stage 2 leader, the top leadership styles are Coaching, Pacesetting and Commanding. A successful leader must be able to bring all three leadership styles into play based on the situation, but in Stage 2, Coaching is the most effective style.

> Leadership development must be the strategic priority of the enterprise.

When you are utilizing a Coaching style, your role is to connect what a person wants with the company's goals. A good coaching leader motivates and enhances employee performance by building long-term capabilities and self-confidence.

A story in *Primal Leadership*, by author Daniel Goleman, emphasizes how effective a Coaching style can be.

She was new at the firm and eight months pregnant. Staying late one night, she looked up from her work and was startled to see her boss standing at her door. He asked how she was doing, sat down and started to talk with her. He wanted to know all about her life. How did she like her job? Where did she want to go in her career? Would she come back to work after she had the baby? These conversations continued daily over the next month until the woman had her baby. The boss was David Ogilvy, the legendary advertising executive. The pregnant newcomer was Shelley Lazarus, now CEO of Ogilvy & Mather, the huge ad agency that Ogilvy founded. One of the main reasons Lazarus says she's still here, decades later, is the bond she forged with mentor Ogilvy in those first after-hour conversations.

Today, Shelley Lazarus is Chairman Emeritus of Ogilvy & Mather. Her love for the company she helped to build and for the man who taught her what running a business is all about is strong to this day.

"Of all the things we talked about, I remember most what he said about people. He said to me: 'You can never spend too much time thinking about, worrying about and caring about your people because, at the end of the day, it's only the people who matter. Nothing else. If you always hire people who are smaller than you are, we shall become a company of dwarfs. If, on the other hand, you always hire people who are bigger than you are, we shall become a company of giants.'"

It is by getting to know your employees on a deeper, more personal level that triggers genuine motivation and superior performance.

WHAT DOES A COACHING STYLE LOOK LIKE?

Coaching leaders not only retain talented people, they build an organization that encourages accountability and transparency. A leader who uses the Coaching style helps employees uncover answers and solutions, identify their unique strengths and their weaknesses and ties them to their personal and career aspirations. They help employees conceptualize a plan for reaching those goals, while being specific about what the leader's responsibility is and what the employee's responsibility is. Coaching isn't hand holding, it's giving someone a hand.

Larry Bossidy, co-author of *Execution: The Art of Getting Things Done*, believes good coaching is about trying to impart experience. In his article, "The Art of Good Coaching," he says, "You try to point out the best way of doing something, not because you are so smart, but because you've seen it 100 times." Bossidy believes that if he helps people find a better way of doing something, he's contributed to their overall success and that's what coaching is all about. Conversely, if your people don't get better, it's your fault too. The article goes on to say, "Coaching and performance are intricately tied." You can get short-term performance by dictating what needs to be done or you can create an environment where people are continually coached to deliver great performance.

Coaching is a two-way street. You need to listen to how people respond. A good coach has great interpersonal skills, is a good communicator and knows when to press and when to praise. You need to tune into people's thoughts and show them how their participation fits into the overall goals of the company.

A Coaching leader is good at delegating and giving employees goals that stretch them, not just tasks that get a job done. This ability to delegate will work to the leader's advantage as the company moves into the next stage of growth. Coaching works best with employees who show initiative and are looking for opportunities to improve. Coaching's surprisingly positive emotional impact stems from the willingness of a leader to communicate a belief in people's potential. Leaders who have a high degree of empathy, who listen first before reacting or giving feedback, often ask themselves, "Is this about my issue or goal or theirs?"

> Coaching isn't hand holding, it's giving someone a hand.

While Coaching is the most effective style, it is also the least used. Patience and a willingness to learn the art of delegation are required to become an effective coach and too often leaders feel the need to solve instead of teach.

In Simon Synek's book, *Start With Why*, he talks about how most companies understand *what* they do. They make sure they have a value proposition that describes *how* they do it, but the challenge for many organizations is helping people understand the *why*. In Synek's research, great leaders work from the inside out and they start with the *why* and make sure every single person in the company understands that w*hy* too. The Coaching style supports this "inside out" approach which is why this style is the most effective tool a leader can bring to their organization.

WHAT DOES A PACESETTING STYLE LOOK LIKE?

Leaders who tend toward a Pacesetting style, focused on high performance, often think they are Coaching when in fact they are micromanaging or simply telling people how to do their jobs. Pacesetting leaders tend to focus on short-term goals, such as sales figures. However, the Pacesetting style shows up in Stage 2 for all the right reasons.

Used sparingly, this style can help set the standard for excellence in an organization, especially if the leader exemplifies that excellence in his or her own actions, not just in words. According to Goleman, "Pacesetting makes sense in particular during the entrepreneurial phase of a company's life cycle, when growth is all important." When a group is highly competent and motivated and needs little direction, this style can be effective.

The challenge for a Pacesetting leader is to know when to back off. Without balancing this style with the highly effective Coaching style, people will quickly lose motivation, especially when faced with a manager who never appears satisfied. Pacesetters tend to be less clear when setting guidelines or expectations. They tend to focus only on the goals or results and can come off as uncaring. This leaves employees feeling pushed too hard or worse, like the leader doesn't trust them. Morale will plummet under a Pacesetting leader and poor performance will become the norm.

To become good at this style a leader must continually find ways to improve performance, which comes with a healthy dose of initiative in seizing opportunities. Becoming competent in new approaches that raises their own performance level and the performance level in those they lead is how Pacesetting becomes a strength and not a weakness.

For a Pacesetting leader their dilemma is that the more pressure they put on people for results, the more anxiety it provokes. When people lose sight of the vision by constantly being driven to only care about results, the exceptional employees will leave. If a leader doesn't work to improve their coaching skills and become better at defining expectations and managing them, sustainable growth will remain elusive.

WHAT DOES A COMMANDING STYLE LOOK LIKE?

In Stage 2, two out of the three leadership styles are called dissonant styles, Pacesetting and Commanding, meaning "apply with caution."

"Do it because I say so" is what the Commanding style looks like. Sometimes called the *coercive style,* it has its place in the quiver of styles but must be used sparingly and never relied upon to grow a sustainable business.

According to the data from Goleman's research, the Commanding style is the least effective of all of the styles as it invariably focuses on what people did wrong rather than what they did well. So why is it even a part of a leader's skill set?

Despite the negative associations, this style is useful in Stage 2 when there's a need to respond to an emergency. An example would be the loss of a large account, which can immediately turn a cash rich company into a struggling startup. If a leader needs to shock people into new ways of thinking and doing in order to keep the company viable, the Commanding style is useful.

Drawing upon this style, a leader must learn to keep her anger and impatience in check, or to use anger artfully to channel outbursts that get instant attention and mobilize people to change or get results. If a leader lacks the self-awareness that helps her manage emotions such as anger, the dangers of the Commanding style are high. A leader who can determine when this style is helpful, is a leader who is emotionally aware and knows how to use the six leadership styles to her advantage.

LEADERSHIP STYLES FOR STAGE 1 AND STAGE 2

STAGE 1 (1 - 10 EMPLOYEES)	STAGE 2 (11-19 EMPLOYEES)
Visionary	Coaching
Coaching	Pacesetting
Commanding	Commanding

WHEN LEADERSHIP STYLE
IS OUT OF ALIGNMENT

The ability to effectively utilize all six leadership styles is what distinguishes an emotionally aware leader from a leader who elects to focus more on tasks than people. Business owners feel a tremendous sense of urgency when launching a new product or service. The pressure forces the leader to be more direct and there can be a tendency to micro-manage in this early stage. A Commanding or Pacesetting style may work in the short term but not in the long term.

When a company moves into Stage 2 and the leadership style is stuck in Pacesetting or Commanding, good people leave and the wrong people stay. In larger organizations, a Pacesetting or Commanding leader can almost fly under the radar, creating mini-cultures of toxic leadership that slowly erode trust. The company will struggle to keep good people. Management tends to believe their own mind script that those who leave "just weren't the right fit." When leaders hide behind their own failings, good companies can become poisonous environments and very rarely recover.

Developing a new leadership style means learning to change how you operate with people. The first step in this journey is to honestly assess your effectiveness today. Leadership development isn't a program, it's a strategic initiative that should permeate a culture and encourage personal development, starting at the top. By understanding all six of the leadership styles and adjusting to each stage of growth, a CEO will be better prepared for the changes that come as the company adds employees.

Take our Leadership Style Assessment (on the next page) to identify your strengths and weaknesses.

LEADERSHIP STYLE ASSESSMENT

Directions: Within each grouping of six statements please select the statement that most represents your leadership style and put the #6 after it. Then select your second choice by assigning it a #5. Then select your third choice by assigning it a #4 and so on until you select your last choice by assigning it a # 1.

A. Your leadership style helps the organization understand where it is going. _____

B. Your leadership style helps people identify their unique strengths and weaknesses and tying those to personal and career aspirations. _____

C. Your leadership style helps people repair broken trust in the organization._____

D. Your leadership style is based on genuinely listening to people. _____

E. Your leadership style is based on a high standard of excellence. _____

F. Your leadership style is based on a decisive commanding presence that people can trust. _____

A. People feel pride in the organization as a result of your values and vision. _____

B. People believe that your advice is genuinely in their best interest. _____

C. People experience greater harmony, better communication and improved morale based on your leadership abilities. _____

D. People believe that you can settle any conflict. _____

E. People feel a drive to improve their performance in your company. _____

F. People under your leadership have clear guidelines and understand what is expected of them. _____

A. As a result of your leadership style people see how their work fits into the big picture. _____

B. As a result of your leadership style people have a sense that you believe in them and that you expect their very best effort. _____

C. As a result of your leadership style people feel they are more important to you than the task they are doing. _____

D. As a result of your leadership style people believe they are really a part of an overall team. _____

E. As a result of your leadership style people feel a need to create new opportunities for the company. _____

F. As a result of your leadership style people feel confident that someone is in charge. _____

YOUR TOP LEADERSHIP STYLE

Thanks for taking the Leadership Styles Assessment. Once you have captured your scores and placed them in the appropriate area below, look at the 'key' section to determine what your top leadership style is based on where you are today. Remember, leadership styles are situational. The value in identifying your leadership style and comparing it with where you are in your stage of growth is to help you understand if your leadership style is a hidden agent that may be hindering your ability to help your company grow.

All "A" statements scores _____+ _____+ _____ = _____

All "B" statements scores _____+ _____+ _____ = _____

All "C" statements scores _____+ _____+ _____ = _____

All "D" statements scores _____+ _____+ _____ = _____

All "E" statements scores _____+ _____+ _____ = _____

All "F" statements scores _____+ _____+ _____ = _____

THE KEY TO YOUR LEADERSHIP STYLES:

A score = Visionary: The Visionary Leader is particularly effective when changes, even a business turnaround, require a new vision or clarifying a new direction. People are motivated by Visionary Leadership toward shared dreams that resonate with a company's values, goals and mission.

B score = Coaching: The Coaching Leader connects what a person wants with the company's goals. A good Coaching Leader motivates and enhances employee performance by building long-term capabilities and self-confidence. It is by getting to know their employees on a deeper, personal level that these leaders make that link a reality.

C score = Affiliative: An Affiliative Leader creates harmony by connecting people to each other, often healing rifts in a team, providing motivation during stressful times or strengthening connections. The focus is on the emotional needs of employees over works goals. This empathy allows a leader to care for the whole person and boosts morale par excellence.

D score = Democratic: A Democratic Leader values people's input and they get commitments through participation. They typically are attuned to a wide range of people and they build consensus when unclear about which direction to take. This often generates fresh ideas for executing it.

E score = Pacesetting: Pacesetting Leaders meet challenging and exciting goals to get high-quality results from a motivated and competent team. These leaders require initiative and the hyper-vigilant readiness to create opportunities to do better and meet goals. This leadership style's continual high pressure performance zone can be debilitating for employees. These leaders typically lack self-awareness or the ability to collaborate or communicate effectively hence employee morale plummets and a total lack of trust ensues.

F score = Commanding: In a crisis, this leadership style can kick-start a turn-around and allay fears by providing crystal clear direction. A Commanding Leader is highly successful at unfreezing useless business habits or ruts and they relentlessly drive for better results. A legacy of the old command-and-control hierarchies that typified 20th century businesses, this military approach is truly appropriate to the battlefield, hospital emergency room or a hostile takeover.

Largest number is your dominant style. Second largest number is your secondary style. Third largest number is your auxiliary style. In case of a tie, you need to declare a preference between the styles.
Based on the work of Daniel Goleman, Richard Boyatzis and Annie McKee, Primal Leadership, Harvard Universit.

Challenge #1: Hiring Quality People

Of course, we all want to hire quality people. The challenge is figuring out what that looks like for you. A perfect fit for my company may not work at all for you. So how do you go about making quality hires?

Let's keep the Gates of Focus in mind as we approach hiring. As stated, the Stage 2 gates are Profit/Revenue first, Process second and People third. So which candidate is going to make your bottom line better? How might you tell? Seek individuals who like a challenge, expect change and would be bored otherwise. Maybe their interests are adrenaline sports like rock climbing, surfing or scuba diving.

If your company is approaching Stage 3 in size, ask yourself if you need a specialist (CFO, Sales Manager, Operations Manager, or Social Media Expert). If that's the case, make sure your team understands how this new person will fit into the grand scheme of things. Reinforce to the specialist that there will be some rocky days ahead and they will need to dig in like everyone else. Setting expectations with your team and new hires is especially important.

Presuming you need a specialist, can you start the person on a part-time basis for the first three months? Hiring the wrong individual can cost at least three times their annual compensation. Taking the time to hire right is truly an investment in the future success of your company.

Your goal with this challenge is to make sure you put the effort, resources and processes in place today to grow toward the future. If this challenge isn't addressed now, in the formative stages of growth, the long lasting effects of hiring the wrong people will impact all aspects of your company. The results will be seen in your culture, your ability to keep customers, your ability to make sustainable profit and your ability to grow.

How to hire the right people is a topic that could fill a warehouse with the books written on the subject. I've included several resources at the end of this book and would urge you to consider them if you are looking for definitive approaches to hiring.

The challenges that go along with hiring the right person begin with these three questions:

1. Do you know what skills are necessary for the position you are hiring for?
2. Do you know what the right person looks like – can you describe them?
3. Do you know what process you should use to find that person?

When I ask CEOs to describe their ideal employee, I get great answers. However, when I ask if these attributes are ever articulated and even more importantly, considered in the hiring process, the answer is usually no.

EXERCISE #1:

KNOW WHAT YOU WANT

As business owners, we are reluctant to ask for what we want when it comes to hiring. We expect our hiring process to be foolproof and we leave a lot to chance. I encourage business owners and the management team to write down the attributes of an exceptional employee.

Here are some characteristics to think about. Add your own and make this list a part of your hiring process. Ask interview questions that uncover these traits.

1. ADAPTABLE

Willing to adjust their plans, resources and beliefs to meet the ever-changing requirements of the enterprise.

2. SELF-CONFIDENT

Having a core sense of self that is wholly independent of outer circumstances and being willing to venture into the unknown with a sense of assurance.

3. ACCOUNTABLE

The willingness to be held responsible for the outcome of some event and/or to the behavior/performance of both themselves and/or to others.

4. PROACTIVE

The initiative to take charge of the moment and discover a solution when one is not readily apparent.

5. INDUSTRIOUS

Committed to the work-of-the-work and following through beyond the logical conclusion of any task.

6. WELL-MEANING

Holding the best intentions for the enterprise and all concerned.

7. OPTIMISTIC

Choosing to infuse the moment with a reality-based, advancing view of a potential outcome.

8. RESOURCEFUL

Able to see beyond the standard application of resources to discover an alternative solution or fresh view of commonly held beliefs and/or behavior.

9. CURIOUS

Continually inquire after the truth to what lays behind the surface of any human experience.

10. PASSIONATE

Infusing the work and the people of the enterprise with an appreciation and intense interest in their advancement.

11. RESPECTFUL

Recognizing and honoring the dignity of the individual as well as the sanctity of the enterprise's interests.

12. INTEGRITY

Doing what they say they will do, when they say they will do it, as well as being uncompromising and congruent with the company's core values.

THE VALUE IN KNOWING
WHAT YOU WANT

Once you are clear about what you are looking for in an employee, you are better able to articulate those attributes in your position description and your employee performance indicators.

Bill Bonnstetter and Ashley Bowers, authors of *Talent Unknown: 7 Ways to Discover Hidden Talent & Skills*, write, "A better way to hire would be to create a process to identify the skills and talents required by the job and then seek an experienced person who has acquired and developed those skills." The authors go on to say that most hiring processes don't assess those skills and talents, leaving it up to the individual to present their case when going through a hiring process and even more challenging, leaving it up to a hiring manager to know what those skills and talents look like.

Think about your own experience as you were developing your career. Can you articulate the skills you now possess based on your experiences? Do you describe what you did, instead of list the skills that allowed you to excel in that position?

The ability to identify learned skills versus job activities is challenging and it's why researching and looking for effective hiring tools is worth a leader's time and effort. For example, in *Talent Unknown*, the authors list the skills a salesperson might have accumulated over time:

Persuasion

Personal accountability

Goal orientation

Presenting

Self-management

Territory management

Customer relations

Diplomacy and tact

Empathy

Flexibility

Competitiveness

Sense of urgency

It's hard for potential job candidates to evaluate the skills learned over time; it's even harder for an employer to know how to describe or test for those skills. Bonnstetter is the CEO of TTI Success Insights (TTISI.com) and has created a company based on his research and study of human behavior. TTISI's assessment tools help managers identify the skills and talents required for a job and uncover those talents and skills in order to hire the right people for the right positions.

EXERCISE #2:

WHAT IT TAKES TO HIRE THE BEST

Lou Adler, best-selling author of *Performance-based Hiring*, shares some tips on how the best hiring managers hire the best people.

Tip #1: Clarify expectations upfront. Create performance-based job descriptions that describe the 4 – 5 critical performance objectives required to be successful in the role.

Tip #2: Refuse to compromise on your demand for hiring top talent. There should be no question that getting the right people on the team is the key to building a successful company.

Tip #3: Fully engage in the recruiting process. Spend more time with candidates before, during and after the interviewing process.

Tip #4: Value potential over experience. In Adler's experience, managers who hired the best people looked for their potential over time, not simply ticking off the skills on a job description.

What system are you using to ensure that you are doing whatever it takes to hire the best? If your hiring process is not intentional and defined, chances are you will struggle to find the best candidates for your company.

According to Verne Harnish's *Mastering the Rockefeller Habits*, "hiring is a numbers game." The companies that attract the best people usually do so because they have a great reputation. He encourages hiring managers to ask these questions: Did we receive a lot of high-quality applications for the last position we hired? Are you selling your company and your vision? You want people attracted to who you are and what you stand for.

Apply the same vigor to your recruiting tactics as you do your lead generation, from writing the job description to crafting the ad. Position your company as a great place to work and seek to differentiate yourself from everyone else.

THE VALUE IN KNOWING WHAT IT TAKES TO HIRE THE BEST

So many business owners rely on gut instinct or select new hires who mirror their own personalities or perceived talents and skills. A little structure brings huge benefits a business. For instance, do you conduct background checks on potential hires who will be performing sensitive jobs? I'm referring to those who will handle money, or could be tempted by inventory. The higher the level of impact, sensitivity or opportunity the position requires, the more intense the level of scrutiny should be.

This isn't the time to wing it. There are valuable and effective tools available and in the reference section of this book you'll find resources worth investigating.

Here are some steps you can take that will help you to better understand what you are looking for when hiring and dramatically increase your ROI per new employee.

STEP 1:

Look around your organization and ask yourself, "What do my best employees do differently? What makes them who they are? What are their attitudes and behaviors?"

STEP 2:

At the same time, evaluate every single job in your company. I mean really sit down and think about:

    a. What exactly does this role bring to my company?

    b. Do I have a well-defined job description in case the person who is currently in that role leaves and I have to rehire?

    c. Does this person's job overlap with any other jobs in the company today?

STEP 3:

Once you have written down all of the key roles, write job descriptions for each one and ask yourself:

    a. Is the right person currently in each role?

    b. If the answer is YES, ask yourself WHY?

    c. If the answer is NO, see if there is another role in the company they are better suited for.

It's your job as the CEO to build a team. Make sure you consciously focus on clarifying roles and responsibilities — that is where 90% of your success rests as you bring new people on board.

EXERCISE #3:

CREATE AN EFFECTIVE HIRING PROCESS

A sensible hiring practice must be established in the early stages of growth. Ensure that your process is documented and available to all hiring managers.

I use a 3-step process that helps identify key aspects of job positions and gets buy-in from the rest of the team. This process was introduced to me when I was a member of a peer advisory group. The speaker was Bob Spence and his system made so much sense that I immediately embraced it. I used it to create job positions that incorporated our values and gathered input from core team members.

Develop specifications for the position. First, **identify your stakeholders**. These are the individuals who have a direct interest in the position and understand the position intimately; the people who will manage or directly report to the position, or who have done or are currently doing well in the position.

Conduct a brainstorming session with the stakeholders to determine the **key performance objectives** for the position. The key performance objectives should focus on the five to six main results (big picture) the position is responsible for. The stakeholders will also complete a job assessment, which will identify the communication style, motivational rewards, personal skills and/or acumen required for superior performance in this position.

Next, **create the job description**. Use the key performance objectives and job assessment results to further clarify the finer details of the position. Ensure you have identified the position's recurring duties and areas of accountability. When employees understand what is required of their position, companies will get a much higher level of performance. The job description should also consider the desired experience, skill sets and previous education/experience required. It should include a description of the working environment, expected travel time, recurring meetings, etc.

Make it as detailed as possible and use it during the onboarding process to outline what will be expected from the employee: the tasks, training courses and additional responsibilities they will be accountable for. Be sure to also review the performance metrics of the position to ensure they include the key performance objectives and other details identified in the job description.

Once the key performance objectives and the job description are complete, be sure to review the entire hiring process from beginning to end.

How does a department identify and get approval for hiring a new employee?

- How and where is the job advertised?
- How do you source for qualified candidates?
- How do you analyze and screen resumes?
- How do you decide which applicants to interview?
- What does your interview process look like? Do you have a defined evaluation system?
- Who conducts the first and second interviews?
- How do you decide which applicants move forward for second interviews, reference checks or background checks?
- How do you decide which candidate to offer the job?

GREAT ALL-PURPOSE INTERVIEW QUESTIONS

Asking great questions is a vital part of the interview process. Broad open-ended questions give a candidate plenty of room to reveal himself and they stimulate discussion. Your goal is to reduce tension and encourage forthright communication. Aim for a relaxed and unpressured pace. Allow silence to be a part of the process. Don't rush in and answer your own questions if the candidate is slow to respond or struggles with an answer. Let the candidate fill in those pauses with his or her own thoughts and answers. First class interviewers encourage candidates to ask questions throughout the interview process.

- How have your past job experiences prepared you directly or indirectly for this position?
- Describe a normal day at your present job ... a busy day ... a great day.
- What did you like most about your last job? What did you like least?
- How do you see this job fitting into your career plans?
- How did the company's philosophy or attitudes affect you and your work?
- How would you describe your previous boss's management style?
- How did you work together?
- What do you require from a boss?
- What kind of people did you have to deal with in your last job?

- What were your least successful relationships? Why?
- What were your specific responsibilities?
- When you have a problem with a co-worker, do you prefer direct confrontation or tact and delicacy?
- How do you make decisions?
- What authority did you have at your last job?
- What improvements did you make?
- Give some examples of situations where you were criticized?
- How did you react and why.

THE VALUE IN CREATING A HIRING PROCESS

A streamlined hiring process is essential to ensuring you hire the highest quality employees who will help your company grow, execute your vision and mission and assimilate seamlessly into your culture.

The hiring process does not end with the new hire. Spend time evaluating your organizational chart and think about what positions you need to help your company grow. It's not uncommon to go through this exercise and recognize a key position is missing, which can cause a bottleneck in workflow. Your people are your best asset and ultimately impact the bottom line more than any other factor in your business.

EXERCISE #4

DEVELOP AN EFFECTIVE ONBOARDING STRATEGY

As a hiring manager, I prided myself on making sure that once a person was hired, we took the time to help them integrate into our company. Our goal was to find the best, show them the ropes, tap into their own experience and continue to build a solid team.

I remember the day our employees awarded my business partner, Sherri, and me with a small plastic bag with 100 pennies in it. We had just celebrated hiring our 100th employee. I still have that bag of pennies on my bookshelf. It was a daunting milestone.

I looked upon the entire hiring process as the most important task of our company. I have many stories about hires gone bad and each time it happened, I felt the loss personally. In the cases where the new hire left within three to six months, I chalked it up to being in too great of a hurry or we didn't do the diligence we should have. However, when we lost a good employee after they had been there a year or more, I knew something wasn't working at the inner core of our company.

In one exit interview with an employee I highly respected, I asked why she was leaving. She didn't mince words: we had a very cliquish culture. It was extremely hard to feel a part of the company. People weren't forthcoming with information. It was just too hard to get work done.

Everyone in our company was onboarded, but not all new hires were onboarded particularly well. After that exit interview, we put some different hiring practices in place and we stopped looking at our orientation process as simply paperwork. We developed management objectives that held our managers accountable for retaining good employees. They had to be much more aware of how new hires were interacting with our existing employees, how effective their teams were performing and they had to work extremely hard to show me how effective our onboarding process was.

Our goal was to help a new hire hit the ground running almost immediately and create a culture that helped them feel connected to our values and our organization. We wanted them to be excited about joining our company.

In the book, *Successful Onboarding*, by Mark Stein and Lilith Christianson, they identify four pillars of the onboarding process. The first pillar is Cultural Mastery. And for this exercise, and because I believe culture is the most defining aspect of any organization, we'll explore ideas on how to help new hires understand the company's culture.

The ability of the company to introduce to new hires what the culture represents and how it is expressed will determine whether that new hire enjoys their new experience or dreads coming to work every day. Too often, culture is assumed to be understood, instead of taught. A company's values are integral to their culture.

Have you identified, articulated and defined your values? I see this exercise ignored all the time. One of the first questions I ask a CEO is "what are your values?" Without a strong set of values, a company will simply go where the wind takes them. Values determine how people will behave.

Because we became too big for me to be involved in hiring every employee, I made it a point to spend thirty minutes with every new hire. I would explain our values, what we cared about, how we treated our customers, how we treated each other. Over the years, we rewarded people when they exhibited those values.

After one of my sessions with a new hire, Wayde, he stood up, shook my hand and said, "It all sounds good Laurie. But in thirty days I'll be back. And if I see what you are talking about, I'll buy you lunch." I was a bit caught off guard as no one had ever challenged me in that way before. Wayde was back in thirty days and he bought me lunch.

Culture is represented in how people treat each other. What behaviors do you encourage and what behaviors are unacceptable? Find opportunities to share examples of how people work together effectively. Make sure new hires experience how your culture encourages all ideas and is open to hearing opposing views.

Have you defined which behaviors you want to see and which behaviors aren't acceptable? What are the unspoken ways that work gets done at your company? These are the interactions that happen during lunch or in the hallway. Without an intentional understanding of these subtle work habits, a new hire can feel intimidated when they stumble upon one of these informal sessions and people suddenly go quiet. How can a new hire become a part of the informal aspects of working at your company?

A company's culture must be defined, not left to chance. If you haven't defined your culture by the time you move into Stage 2, don't wait another day. Everyone will feel better, work better and behave better once they know and understand the vision, mission and core values. Once you know what that culture is, find opportunities every day to share examples of how that culture "shows up" with everyone. If your culture is a living, breathing entity, it will be easier to introduce it to new hires.

THE VALUE OF DEVELOPING AN EFFECTIVE ONBOARDING PROCESS

Onboarding came into vogue in 1999 and is now enjoying a renewed popularity. With all the talk about disengaged employees, it's about time we, as business owners, started paying more attention to the process of hiring quality people. That process has to be more than a week of learning how to use a new computer, filling out paperwork and going to lunch with selected employees.

Kick off your own onboarding redesign with a serious diagnosis of what you currently do, how you do it, what's working and what isn't. To do that you need to talk to the new members of your team and find out what would have made their experience of joining your company more fulfilling. I would caution against just picking up the latest onboarding book and simply implementing the steps outlined. Create your own process; you have all the tools you need. You have experienced staff members who can act as mentors. You have data that tells you that it will cost you three times that person's salary to

> Everyone will feel better, work better and behave better once they know and understand the vision, mission and core values.

replace them. You believe that people are your greatest asset. What are you waiting for?

RESOLVING THE CHALLENGE OF HIRING QUALITY PEOPLE

Effective leaders are always on the lookout for good people. Recruiting for talent should be an ongoing activity. As a Stage 2 company with 11 – 19 employees, you are starting to look for people that bring a specific set of experiences to the table. In Stage 1, your hiring decisions were about the fit. In Stage 2, you need to find people who have the skills and talents that support what your company needs to improve revenue and profits. That's why it's so critical for you to understand where your company is going and what type of people you need to take you there.

In the book, *Why CEOs Fail*, by Dotlich and Cairo, they define leadership as "the capacity to build and maintain a high-performing team." They also believe that "leadership should be evaluated in terms of the performance of the team." There really isn't anything more important that a leader can focus on then hiring and retaining exceptional employees.

There's no doubt about it; hiring and managing people is challenging. Business owners tend to look for people who appear on the surface to be a lot like them. Meaning, they come across as confident, capable and willing to do whatever it takes to get a job done. These characteristics describe an entrepreneur, not an employee. Employees live in a different world than business owners. They are not wired the same way and tend to want more structure and direction. An entrepreneur might rail against processes because they slow things down, but an employee needs processes to perform well.

In John Maxwell's book, *The 21 Laws of Effective Leadership*, he references the Law of Magnetism, which states, "who you are is who you attract." If you are clear about the strengths of your organization and promote them clearly, you'll attract candidates with similar strengths.

Challenge #2: Expanding Sales

E ven though you are no longer a startup, expanding sales remains a critical focus for a Stage 2 owner. Having identified your value proposition in Stage 1, Stage 2 is about delivering on it and growing a healthy top line revenue stream. You should have also identified the problem you are solving for your customers and have a clear perspective on your role as it pertains to the sales process.

The key to this challenge is to FOCUS on the sales process. FOCUS on what it is you are selling. FOCUS on why you are selling it and FOCUS on how it will solve your customers' problems.

I believe successful companies are those where the CEO has taken the time to immerse herself in the problem solving aspects of her product or service and is able to articulate those problem-solving aspects to potential customers. If the CEO can do this, she can teach others to do it.

For ideas on how to develop a value proposition, the five steps of the buying decision, the seven steps of the sale and how to create marketing messages, I refer you to my book, *Survive and Thrive: How to Unlock Profits in a Startup with 1 – 10 Employees.*

In Stage 2, expanding sales must move beyond the basics. Now it's time to fully engage in the selling process, which becomes a bigger challenge in this stage for the following reasons:

1. You've created demand for your products or services and now you have to perfect the delivery of those products and services.
2. In the scurry of delivering to customers, you allow your sales to languish, with the belief that you just need to work on the execution side of your business.

How you think about the relationship you want to establish with your customers is vitally important to expanding sales.

The data giant, Satmetrix, presents these interesting statistics:

- Acquiring a new customer can cost 5 – 7 times more than retaining current customers.
- An average company loses 10% of its clients annually.
- A 2% increase in customer retention has the same bottom line effect as cutting costs by 10%.
- A 5% reduction in customer defection rates can increase profits up to 25 – 65%, depending upon the industry.

By recognizing the importance of keeping existing customers more than just satisfied – in fact, keeping them delighted – should be the goal of every organization.

Developing a culture of *customer-centric thinking* helps an organization stay on top of customers' needs and allows them to believe that you are a strategic partner, not just another vendor. In Adrian Slywotsky's book, *The Profit Zone*, he suggests three phases that show how customer-centered thinking changes as a company grows.

THE COMPANY-CENTRIC PHASE

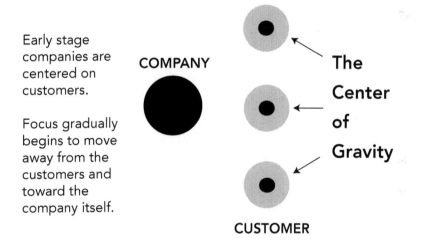

Early stage companies are centered on customers.

Focus gradually begins to move away from the customers and toward the company itself.

COMPANY

The Center of Gravity

CUSTOMER

The Profit Zone, A. Slywotsky

THE GROWTH PHASE

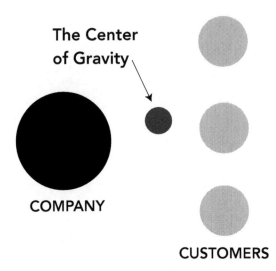

The Center of Gravity

COMPANY

CUSTOMERS

As the company grows bigger, the center of gravity moves even more toward the company, away from the customer.

The Profit Zone, A. Slywotsky

THE COMPANY-CENTRIC PHASE

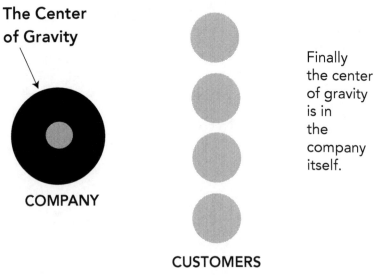

The Center of Gravity

COMPANY

CUSTOMERS

Finally the center of gravity is in the company itself.

The Profit Zone, A. Slywotsky

Clearly, it becomes harder to maintain focus on the customer as your company grows beyond your span of control. That's why creating a customer-centric mindset that permeates your company should start now.

But more importantly, you have to spend time in your own head figuring out how your product or service solves your target audience's problems. This doesn't have to be costly or complicated. It just has to have your energy around it.

EXERCISE #1:

EXPLORE CUSTOMER EXPECTATIONS

As you ramp up for growth, recognize the importance of a customer-centered approach to marketing, sales and delivery to stay grounded. Remember, customers become satisfied when their expectations are met; they become loyal when their expectations are exceeded.

Your first challenge is to determine what those expectations are and then knock them out of the park. So, let's explore how you first determine expectations.

I'll share a story about an experience in which my expectations were not met and the repercussions. At a local restaurant, my husband and I and a few friends waited a full hour to be served our meal. The restaurant wasn't crowded and we had made reservations. Needless to say, that wasn't my expectation when I walked in. As the grumbling from my guests confirmed, it wasn't theirs either.

My expectation is in line with a study a famous restaurant in New York conducted that showed customers spent, on average, 65 minutes from the time they sat until they finished their dessert. So, we complained. The manager offered free desserts. The fact that we were not happy about waiting so long to eat our main meal should have alerted this manager that asking us to wait on another portion of our meal was not a good plan. We asked for him to comp our bottle of wine. His unbelievable response was, "We don't make any money on wine."

> Customers become satisfied when their expectations are met; they become loyal when their expectations are exceeded.

I'm pretty sure this restaurant had not had the discussion about what expectations they should exceed when it comes to serving their customers.

Problems are going to show up in any business. You know at some point you will disappoint a customer. The worst thing you can do is be unprepared to deal with it proactively. Your intent should be to establish a standard acknowledgement, "Yes, we messed up. Here's how we will take care of it so that our customers walk away satisfied that their concerns were heard."

We aren't going to go back to that restaurant. Admittedly, the lack of our business alone in not going to impact the profits of one restaurant, but you know, we take every chance we get to tell that story. And we mention the name of the restaurant. In a report by allbusiness.com, satisfied customers tell nine people how happy they are. Dissatisfied customers tell 22 people about a bad experience.

According to the website retentionofcustomers.com, 68% of customers leave because they perceive indifference. The manager at our local restaurant wasn't just indifferent; he let us know that he cared more about his profit margin then he did about our satisfaction.

Seth Godin is a familiar guru on all things marketing. He explains that we categorize our sales and non-sales transactions into three categories:

1. I'm doing you a favor.
2. This guy is doing me a favor.
3. This is a favorless transaction.

According to this way of thinking, problems arise when one person in the transaction thinks they are doing the other guy a favor. The remedy, Godin says, is to "always act as if the other guy is doing the favor." That manager would still have two loyal customers if he had simply acted as if we were doing him a favor by coming to his restaurant.

Here are some questions you should be able to answer to help your company close the gap between what your customers expect and what you deliver.

1. **What can your customer expect from you?** What will you deliver, how often, with what type of attitude and to whom?

2. **What do you need your customer to do?** Tell you when and why they are not happy; tell you what does make them happy.

3. **Do you test to see if your value proposition is clear?** This is easy. After a customer has

experienced your product or service, pick up the phone and ask them if you delivered on your value proposition.

4. **How will you understand your customer's point of view?** You won't if you don't walk a mile in their shoes. This isn't about what you do; it's about how your customer responds to what you do. Take the time to explore their perspective with regard to every aspect of your product or service.

5. **Are there ways to ensure you don't over-promise and under-deliver?** Clarifying expectations throughout the delivery of the product or service ensures that misunderstandings are dealt with in the moment.

6. **Are you able to identify issues before they become issues?** Employee training needs to include how to deal with the "what ifs" of your product or service.

   - What if your product is faulty upon installation?

   - What if you are late delivering a critical service?

   - What if a breaker blows during dinner rush?

   - What if a flood takes out your computer system?

Being able to prepare for the worst helps you to think about always delivering the best.

THE VALUE IN EXPLORING CUSTOMER EXPECTATIONS

Everyone has a set of expectations that begin and end from where they sit, not from where someone else sits.

In Stage 1, you worked hard to introduce people to your products and services. In Stage 2, you don't only want to find new customers; you want to make sure the ones you have are happy. Staying on top of how your customers feel about your product or service will go a long way in helping you understand why they love what you do and how you do it. It's that knowledge that you want to be able to teach each and every new employee. Exceeding expectations isn't just luck; it's a well-defined, well-articulated approach that defines how you do business.

An effective way to secure customer feedback includes a sales follow up interview. This can be done by phone or with an online survey. Here are some topics to explore:

a. What was the client's perception of the Value Proposition as it related to their experience?

b. How did the customer feel they were treated during the sales process?

c. Are they aware of the follow up support offered?

d. Are they experiencing any challenges you should be aware of?

e. Would they recommend the company to one of their friends or business associates?

EXERCISE #2:

FOCUS ON THE THREE PILLARS OF REVENUE GENERATION

There are only three ways to generate revenue in any business:

1. Increase the number of transactions
2. Increase the frequency of the transaction
3. Increase the transaction amount

That's it. A solid marketing plan followed by an intentional sales plan will help you generate revenue. It's very easy in Stage 2 to get caught up in the activity of marketing and sales and ignore the need for a solid plan.

ONE:

INCREASE THE NUMBER OF TRANSACTIONS - FOCUS ON THE CUSTOMER'S INTEREST

Businesses tend to start thinking about generating revenue as it equates to identifying the right target market, determining what that audience wants and creating the value proposition around their product or service in order to sell it. When it comes right down to it, increasing the number of transactions is all about marketing and sales.

In a Stage 2 company, often a formal sales process that starts with lead generation and ends with customer reconnaissance doesn't exist. That's because the company is still CEO-centric and the business owner is still the lead sales person. Their ability to sell is based on their familiarity with their product or service and their focus is not about creating a sales process that can be replicated.

Unfortunately at this stage, marketing is often left to chance, or poorly executed strategies that waste time and money. Sometimes the simple question, "How many leads will it take for us to generate our revenue goal?" is overlooked. Lead generation must drive where your top line revenue will come from. Without a formal process for discovering, capturing and nurturing leads (a marketing process), your sales efforts will be like a boat without a rudder. You can stay afloat, but you have no control over where you go.

REVENUE GENERATORS FOR INCREASING THE NUMBER OF TRANSACTIONS

Define, Create and Implement a Strong Marketing Process: A target customer profile, differentiated messaging and a lead generation process.

Capture and Replicate an Effective Sales Process: Creating rapport, setting expectations, defining the customer's pain, addressing the pain with your solution, a conversation about the budget, asking for a decision and follow up.

Clarify and Explain the Value Transfer: An intentional approach to showing how your solution provides value through the use of testimonials, comparables and value messaging.

TWO:
INCREASE THE TRANSACTION FREQUENCY - STRIVE FOR CUSTOMER LOYALTY

According to Adrienne Zoble, a well-known marketing expert, "A sales call to an existing client or customer costs 15% of what a sales call costs to a prospect." In her book, *The Do-able Marketing Plan*, she says, "Business is all about long-term relationships. When you call to offer congratulations or inquire about an ailing relative or a new baby, without being commercial in any way, you impress your clients big time."

How well do you strive to really stay connected to your customers? Do your customers know all that you offer? Many times, customers will go looking for other products or services that are within your ability to deliver. Take the time to explain your full range of offerings in a detailed conversation at the outset. By making sure your company is diligent in gathering and tracking product or service use feedback, customer business updates, personal information and market information, you ensure a strong ability to increase your transaction frequency. A company's opportunity to increase top line revenue increases substantially when it has disciplined and clear "after the sale" follow through communication with the customer.

REVENUE GENERATORS FOR INCREASING TRANSACTION FREQUENCY

Intentionally Design Your Customer Staircase: Determine your low-end and high-end product/service range, the product/service sequence and the lifetime value of your customer.

Identify and Commit to Customer Reconnaissance: Create and train people on an effective customer inquiry process, install a customer relationship management database and constantly refresh your customer user pool to clear out non-users and make room for your valued customers.

Create a Culture of Value Immersion: Understand how your customers define value, look for new ways to deliver value, identify the value recognition patterns, clarify and test your customer follow through messaging and train staff on what your "best of best" focus on customers looks like.

THREE:
INCREASE THE TRANSACTION AMOUNT - IMPROVE CUSTOMER AWARENESS

"Our clients will complain if we raise our prices." This is the single most common objection voiced by business owners when pressed to raise prices. One CEO was so convinced he would have a client rebellion on his hands, it took a day-long session and his entire staff forcing the issue to raise his prices 10%. In a follow up call a month after the price increase, the CEO sheepishly admitted that not one customer had complained. At the end of the year, his bottom line said it all.

Perception is reality. If your customers perceive value in your products and services because of your dedication to customer service, your fail safe quality control processes and your integrity to fix every wrong and make it right, then pricing will not be an issue.

There are ways to increase the transaction amount that require nothing more than a little creative thinking. Bundling allows you to combine two or more products or services and offer them at an

> **Perception is reality.**

attractive price point. It also changes the perception of the product in the customer's mind; bundling *adds perceived value* and *increases the price.*

Upselling, a sales strategy where you provide opportunities for customers to purchase additional products or services to make a larger sale, is an effective approach and communicates your ability to increase value. Think about upselling this way: The *easiest person* to sell more products to is your current customer. Right? The *easiest time* to sell more products is at the time your customer is buying from you. Right? Conclusion: Your customers are never more willing to buy more than at the time of purchase.

Many companies miss this opportunity because they haven't established what additional offerings would look like. The sales person is left to throw in a bonus to make the sale, which might be a good short-term approach, but is not beneficial in the long term.

But, increasing your prices to simply increase your bottom line could backfire. Eliminate the risk by having a solid plan to communicate the value of your offerings to your clients on an on-going basis.

REVENUE GENERATORS FOR INCREASING TRANSACTION AMOUNT

Identify Bundling Opportunities: Evaluate what you can do to offer higher value with existing products or services. Clarify and Communicate Quality: Continue to fine-tune your messaging to ensure that customers understand the value of your products or services.

Consider Creative Sales Strategies: Identify which products or services lend themselves to upselling or cross-selling opportunities.

10 CRITICAL QUESTIONS TO INCREASE TOP LINE REVENUE

1. Are you satisfied with the results from your company's lead generation efforts over the past six months?

2. Does your company have a structured and proven step-by-step sales process?

3. Does your company successfully combine its products/services into bundled packages that communicate a greater combined value then if they were sold individually?

4. Is your company adept at creating custom combinations of your products and services to meet your customer's unique needs?

5. Can your company communicate quality as a means of upgrading a purchase?

6. Do your customers clearly understand the full range of your product/service pricing?

7. Is your company focused on gathering and tracking key customer feedback?

8. Does your everyday product/service pricing communicate extraordinary value to the customer?

9. Does your sales presentation effectively use powerful client testimonials to improve the closing ratio in your sales process?

10. Is your company particularly successful at communicating to the customer what it is best at delivering?

· ·

7 WAYS TO IMPROVE REVENUE

1. Have a minimum of three – five different revenue streams
2. Purchase direct without a middleman
3. Let someone else be the delivery system for your products to your customers
4. Sell to other people's customers
5. Broaden the range of use for your products and/or services
6. Lengthen the reach of your products and/or services
7. Participate in commissions paid for products or services sold to your customer (affiliate programs)

· ·

THE VALUE OF FOCUSING ON THE THREE PILLARS OF REVENUE GENERATION

Within each of the three categories of increasing top line revenue, there are three critical elements to focus your marketing and sales teams around to capture market share, make sales and maintain strong customer ties.

Be very intentional in how you identify, communicate and implement the three ways to increase revenue in your company. In doing so, you will immediately capture the attention of your marketing and sales team and the rest of your company. You will also create a language of growth and maintain focus by continuing to discuss revenue generation.

EXERCISE #3:

PRACTICE YOUR PITCH

I stood in the doorway while my husband talked to the two young women who had stopped just beyond our porch gate. I knew they were selling something. I was just about to tell them we weren't interested when I overheard one of them say, "We are raising money to go to school in order to better ourselves. We thought you would respect our approach, right?"

One of them actually said, "We know it's annoying to have someone knock on your door and disturb you in your own home, so if we can just explain our program, we promise to be quick."

Both young women were well dressed, personable and confident. I stepped outside while Keisha, the shorter of the two, engaged my husband in a conversation all about him. What did he do? How long had he lived in Tucson? Did he like retirement? She mentioned that her dream was to someday start her own business and my husband pointed to me and said, "She runs her own business."

The women turned their attention toward me and asked what I did, how long had I been doing it, and what were some of the challenges I faced as a woman in business. Each time they asked a question, they also shared a little bit about their dreams and goals and why they were going door-to-door selling magazine subscriptions.

Before long, we were laughing, sharing stories, talking about business ideas, cactus (they were enthralled with a certain cactus in our neighborhood that looked like it had a beard – how engaging is that?), Marsha's children (she had three and was a single mom) and how badly she wanted to provide them with a good home. She knew she would have to earn a better living in order to do that.

Needless to say, my husband and I both bought subscriptions. Like many of us, I hate being "sold" anything. But, these two young women were able to connect with and engage both my husband and me in a short time with a sincere and transparent statement, "we just want to improve ourselves." As they walked away, I thought to myself, whoever trained these two young women was extremely good and kudos to them for practicing their delivery. They were masterful in delivering their pitch.

According to Daniel Pink in his book, *To Sell is Human*, "The purpose of a pitch isn't necessarily to move others immediately to adopt your idea. The purpose is to offer something so compelling that it begins a conversation, brings the other person in as a participant, and eventually arrives at an outcome that appeals to both of you."

What's your pitch? Daniel Pink transformed what once was a dirty word and elevated it to a new level of sophistication. "One out of every nine Americans works in sales." He has also identified six pitches well worth mastering.

The One-Word Pitch – Developed as a concept by Maurice Saatchi, of the famous advertising firm, this strategy touts "one-word equity." The world is populated with "digital natives" – those under 30 who were brought up with the Internet who have almost no attention span. Businesses must vie for recognition by "defining the one characteristic they want most associated with their brand." For example, when someone says "search" we think of Google or when someone says "priceless" we think of MasterCard. What is your one-word pitch that defines your brand?

> One out of every nine Americans works in sales.

The Question Pitch – Studies show that questions can outperform statements but businesses underuse this linguistic tool. Questions are powerful in communication because they immediately bring us into a conversation; they make us think and work a bit harder to respond. When people come up with their own reasons for agreeing or not agreeing with something, they endorse that belief more strongly and tend to act upon it. The next time you are in front of a prospect, ask them a question instead of making a statement and watch the conversation shift.

The Rhyming Pitch –Rhymes boost what linguists and cognitive scientists call "processing fluency" – the ease with which our minds slice, dice and make sense of stimuli. We all remember the nursery rhymes from our childhood. That's because rhymes taste great and go down easily. "Takes a licking and keeps on ticking" is a timeless marketing slogan by Timex, or Stage 2, good for you!

The Subject Line Pitch – Because email is so ingrained in our daily lives, we're not even aware that every email we send is a pitch. It's an invitation to engage, to create a relationship, to get someone's attention. We usually open email if it's from someone we know, but what grabs your attention and gets you to open an email from a stranger?

According to a study by Carnegie Mellon University in 2011, it comes down to utility and curiosity. In their experiment, they used the think-aloud method, where participants worked through their email inboxes and narrated their decisions about what they would read, forward, reply to or delete. They tended to read emails that directly affected their work and to open messages when they had moderate levels of uncertainty about the contents or when they were curious about the message.

People opened messages if they felt they had something to gain or lose. They opened other messages out of simple curiosity. As a result, the Carnegie Mellon researchers found that your email subject lines should be either obviously useful (found the best, found the cheapest, etc.) or intriguing (Engage vs. Rage – learn how to love your employees), but not both.

Along with utility and curiosity a third principle was uncovered: specificity. Brian Clark of Copyblogger, a popular copywriting website, recommends that subject lines be ultra specific. For example, "Prove your golf swing" is less effective than "4 tips to improve your golf swing this afternoon" or "3 simple steps that will improve your bottom line in 30 days."

The Twitter Pitch – We saw this one coming. Twitter has completely changed how people communicate. One of the pioneers of the Twitter pitch is Stowe Boyd, a programmer, designer and investor. In Pink's book, he explains how in 2008, Boyd was heading to a conference to meet with some startup companies. Any entrepreneur who wanted to meet with him had to deliver his pitch via Twitter, now known as the "twit-pitch."

An effective tweet engages recipients and encourages them to take the conversation further. The types of tweets with the lowest ratings fall into three categories: complaints (My plane is late again!), me now (I'm getting ready to take a shower) and presence maintenance (Good morning, everyone!).

The highest rated tweets are those with questions, those that provide information and those that include useful information, even if it is self-promoting.

The Pixar Pitch – Pixar Animation Studios opened in 1979. At the time, it was a geeky computer graphics division of Lucasfilm. Today, it's one of the most successful studios in movie history. While there are many reasons for its success, Emma Coats, a former story artist at the studio, created a template for an irresistible new kind of pitch. She says it's a deep structure of storytelling that involves six sequential sentences:

> Once upon a time ...
> Every day ...
> One day ...
> Because of that ...
> Because of that ...
> Until finally ...

This story line is developed and told over and over again in every movie that Pixar has released. Pink shares the example from the plot of *Finding Nemo*:

"Once upon a time there was a widowed fish named Marlin who was extremely protective of his only son, Nemo. Every day, Marlin warned Nemo of the ocean's dangers and implored him not to swim too far away. One day, in an act of defiance, Nemo ignores his father's warnings and swims into the open water. Because of that, he is captured by a diver and ends up as a pet in the fish tank of a dentist in Sydney. <u>Because of that</u>, Marlin sets off on a journey to recover Nemo, enlisting the help of other sea creatures along the way. <u>Until finally</u>, Marlin and Nemo find each other, reunite and learn that love depends on trust."

Don't dismiss this creative approach to telling your story. Creating your own movie magic to engage people in learning who you are and what you do is a good tactic.

My magazine seller's pitch was essentially a less sophisticated version of the Pixar Pitch. They wove a bit of "once upon a time" into explaining who they were, where they came from, why they were doing what they were doing and what they hoped the happy ending would be.

THE VALUE OF PRACTICING YOUR PITCH

Gurus like Dale Carnegie advised us to be able to master the elevator pitch; the ability to explain who you are and what you do to the poor person trapped in the elevator with you as you rode between floors. The elevator pitch has been standard operating procedure for decades, but as our world has changed, so has the way we communicate.

The McKinsey Global Institute estimates that "the typical American hears or reads more than one hundred thousand words every day." We have so many more distractions; we need to broaden our repertoire of pitches to reach the attention span of the challenged masses.

As I reviewed the six pitches so artfully outlined in Pink's book, I was compelled to apply them to my own world as a business advisor. They aren't easy to create. They require you to seriously think about your work, the outcomes you want to deliver and how you want to be remembered. As with all marketing efforts, they should be a work in progress. If we meet at some point in the future, know that you might well be the recipient of one!

The One-Word Pitch: Complexity!

The Question Pitch: Are you running your business or is it running you?

The Rhyming Pitch: To know is to grow.

The subject line pitch: When being visionary isn't valuable

The Twitter Pitch: Confidence or caution? Which one is running your company today?

The Pixar Pitch: <u>Once upon a time</u>, there was a young woman who thought she would always be working in the career she loved. <u>One day</u>, she was fired and didn't know what else she could do. She ran into a good friend and they decided to start a business. <u>Because of that</u>, they started helping companies communicate messages and created a culture that valued the strengths of their employees. <u>Because of that,</u> she founded her own company and took the lessons she learned and turned them into business practices. <u>Until finally</u>, she became known as a business growth specialist and now helps other business owners understand that their people are their business, that profits should be protected and that growth needs to be managed.

My challenge to you: pick up Pink's book. Go to chapter 7 and run the pitch drill. It's fun. It's educational. It's effective.

RESOLVING THE CHALLENGE OF EXPANDING SALES

It doesn't matter how many sales people you hire or how much you might hate sales, as the owner of a business, you have to keep your eye on sales or the company will fail. With so many things demanding your attention in Stage 2, an increasing level of complexity and 11-19 employees to worry about, it's not uncommon to focus on operations over sales. Keep your eyes on the prize during this critical time in your company's growth spurt.

Although the shift from Stage 1 to 2 is subtle, a lot has changed. The payroll is larger and with more staff comes more equipment. With more equipment comes more maintenance. The cost of doing business is on the rise.

Never forget who your customers are and why they came to you in the first place. When you allow a customer to become a number and not a face, your entire organization suffers. While sales are needed to drive profit, profit should not be the only goal behind sales. Make sure every single person in your company knows the bigger purpose behind what you do. Make it a priority to remind your staff every day that your customers are the lifeblood of the business and to that end, each and every customer must be treated as if they were your last.

> Never forget who your customers are and why they came to you in the first place.

Challenge #3: Continual Cash Flow Challenges

Continual cash flow challenges suck the energy and efforts from otherwise well-run companies. They make companies compromise, qualify, stretch the truth and kid themselves of the real solutions to this urgent issue.

Sixty-five percent of businesses that fail are profitable. This disturbing statistic alone should cause business owners to wake up and pay attention to cash flow. I found this interesting fact in Robert Fleury's book, *The Small Business Survival Guide*. He also points out that "the time required for a business to reach the success level is five to seven years."

By the time you have reached Stage 2, you've learned several lessons. Most business owners, however, are disconnected from the financial side of their business. They rely too heavily on their accountant and believe that if anything were wrong, they'd hear about it.

According to a report by Pat Burr and Richard Heckmann, two small business administration officials, "the most staggering cause for failure is a general lack of managerial skills." A quick summary of their report highlights some common pitfalls:

- Poor site selection
- No financial projections
- Lack of established financial relations
- Offering long-term credit to new customers
- No budget for the first few difficult months
- Relative ignorance in handling financial matters
- Laxity in submitting financial statements to banks
- Uncontrollable urge to invest in long-term commitments

All of these points have roots in poor cash management. A business owner has to have a close relationship with the financial side of their business, or the odds are strongly against long-term success.

In Fleury's opinion, every business owner must develop financial navigation skills, including how to create profit and loss statements, generate a cash analysis report, maintain a balance sheet and have a thorough understanding of the company's record system. While I'm more of a believer in hiring an exceptional bookkeeper during these early stages, I don't disagree with Fleury on the need to educate yourself about the financial side of your business.

As we grew the marketing communications company I helped manage, I remember manually keeping track of each and every invoice that went out, how much it was for, when it was due and noting when it came in. I balanced our checking account every month and

I kept track of cash flow weekly because we were hiring people pretty quickly and I knew we had to have cash available to make payroll.

By Stage 2, you have a lot more cash to manage and the need to manage it well increases. An experienced bookkeeper is a smart hire. The CEO doesn't have to be an expert in financial software, but she does need to understand the financial side of her business.

Trust is a common deterrent to bringing in outside help, especially since there are hundreds of examples of business owners getting ripped off and losing thousands of dollars to unethical individuals. In most cases, these incidents happen because the business owner is completely checked out of the finances. Never abdicate complete financial authority to anyone, under any circumstances, regardless of the size of your business. Ultimately, the financial stability of the organization is the CEO's responsibility, and how that responsibility is handled requires education and literacy.

In Stage 1, you learned how to manage cash flow and create a profit plan (budget). These two processes help protect your cash and provide a forecasting tool that will keep you out of trouble as you grow. In Stage 2, you have to generate more cash, use it wisely and stay on top of every single financial aspect of your business. Delegating means finding experienced financial people to help you manage it.

> Never abdicate complete financial authority to anyone, under any circumstances, regardless of the size of your business.

EXERCISE #1:

GET YOUR FINANCIAL TEAM IN PLACE

Soon after I was fired from a job I loved, I met up with my friend Sherri, who had started a public relations business. We had known each other from our previous careers. Her small company had gained some traction and on the day I joined her at her office in her house, I looked around for something to do. I found a stack of unopened bank statements.

If you have ever been fired from a job, you will recognize the subtle changes a person undergoes after that humiliating experience. For me, in the span of six months, I had gotten divorced, lost my dad and been fired from a successful career I had spent 14 years building. To say I was suffering from a lack of self-confidence would be an understatement. I cautiously walked into Sherri's office and asked quietly, "Would you like me to open these bank statements and reconcile them?"

She looked up and, to her credit, said what I needed to hear, "Laurie, you have a brain. You don't have to ask for permission. Do what you think needs to get done."

My first job became managing the invoices, the payables, the cash flow and making sure we had money in the bank. This came easily to me. As the Superintendent of Recreation for a city in Northern Colorado, I had a substantial budget to manage. I found balancing our small company's bank account highly enjoyable. Soon, however, we were bringing in more revenue and starting to hire more people.

With the needs of an expanded payroll, taxes and my priorities shifting to managing client projects, we needed to hire a bookkeeper.

That single decision is the main reason our small startup grew to over $500,000 in sales in just one year. Putting the responsibility of the financials in the hands of an experienced bookkeeper allowed Sherri and I to focus on growing the business.

Our bookkeeper, Bettie, taught us the value of billable hours, cost of goods, managing overhead and how to never count on sales until the check had cleared the bank. She made sure we knew exactly what was going on financially and insisted we pay attention to payables and receivables. We were well trained to be aware of how much we were paying people and how large our overhead was getting.

In three years, we had grown from 2 to 12 employees and $836,531 in sales. Bettie created profit plans that allowed us to look ahead and project the critical "what ifs":

- What if we didn't land a contract?
- What if we lost a client?
- What if we **did** land a contract?
- What if we hired another project manager in a month?

She taught us that staying on top of the financial side of our business wasn't an option; it was the only way we were going to stay profitable and grow.

Every growing business needs an experienced bookkeeper who does more than simply track your cash and reconcile your bank account. That person can become your most trusted source of financial understanding, so take time to find this crucial team member.

For an in-depth, free report on best practices when hiring a book-keeper, follow this link: http://destination-greatness.com/files/destination-greatness/Bonus-How-To-Hire-A-Bookkeeper.pdf

We also established a good relationship with a banker early on because we needed a credit line. We had landed a couple of contracts that required us to move into larger space, take on a five-year lease and buy more equipment. We took our financials to Bob at one of the national chain banks in Boulder, Colorado.

I remember that first meeting well. Bob asked us about our business, what we did, who our clients were and what our long-term strategy was. We were pretty confident in our answers. Cash flow was solid, receivables were strong, payables were up to date. Then he started asking us questions that went much deeper than the standard overall picture layer. Those next level questions changed how we looked at the growth of our business from that day on.

- How big did we want to get?
- How many employees would we have in a year?
- What was our net profit goal?
- What was our unit of sale?
- How were we tracking our costs?
- What was our current liquidity ratio?
- What was our quick ratio?
- What was our return on assets?
- What was our debt to equity?

We received our first line of credit for $50,000. Bob's advice was to use it as needed but to pay it down as quickly as possible. That line eventually grew to $100,000 and it provided us needed capital as we continued to grow.

We stayed with Bob for 14 years. He always provided solid insight, firm but friendly advice and was there for us during the good times and the bad. Over the years, Bob's career took him to different banks, but we followed him wherever he went. Our relationship was with him, not the bank. He taught us the value of managed growth, understood our business and was always there to answer our questions.

Successful business owners know they need to surround themselves with trusted advisors and people who have expertise in specific areas of the business. In addition to a bookkeeper and a banker, an experienced CPA and an attorney are also critical team members.

Here are some of the criteria you should look for when building your team of trusted financial advisors:

1. Capable of transferring information that may be new to you into information you can use and understand.

2. Ask good questions and are intentional about understanding not only what you do, but why you are doing it. They need to believe in what you are trying to build.

3. Accessible and approachable. You should never feel intimidated or made to feel stupid about questions you ask or issues you bring up.

4. Experts at what they do with a proven track record of results.

THE VALUE OF GETTING YOUR FINANCIAL TEAM IN PLACE

Having an experienced financial team on board in the early stages of growth will keep you focused on the bottom line. Don't assume that you can handle all of the financial aspects of running your business alone. That presumption can quickly lead to disappointment.

An experienced bookkeeper helps you stay on top of payables, receivables, cost of goods, salary issues and overhead creep. In our case, Bettie helped us keep our prices in line with our costs. She also provided hard-to-ignore facts to consider before hiring a new employee or accepting more work. Essentially, she saved us a pile of money and protected us from making costly mistakes.

A smart business owner once told me that I needed to have a close, professional relationship with both a banker and a CPA. The expert advice and counsel of these professionals is invaluable. The more they know about your business, the more invested they become in your personal success.

Avoid the common financial, legal and tax pitfalls that unhinge so many businesses when they are just starting out. And above all, learn from the professionals you gather around you. Knowledge is power and cash flow is king!

EXERCISE #2:

CASH MANAGEMENT AND ANALYSIS

In Stage 1, a simple cash flow management plan was necessary to keep track of how much cash was coming in and going out on any given week. By Stage 2, cash management planning becomes even more important and requires devoted attention. With 11 – 19 employees and revenues exceeding $1,000,000 (in most cases), the practice of cash analysis becomes mandatory. Forecast your cash needs and review how your cash was spent on a regular basis.

As a business owner, you have to find tools, resources and advice that makes sense to you. Don't buy into every financial theory or system you read or hear about. Cash analysis is only a worthwhile tool if it helps *you* manage *your* cash.

A while back, I participated in a CEO peer advisory group. I was the only female in the group and the level of financial testosterone was overwhelming. My peers delighted in coming up with financial evaluations and ratios that they summarized during the "updates" portion of the meeting. They quoted their profit growth in percentages, in all sorts of time frames (daily, weekly, quarterly) and analyzed their cash flows every which way to Sunday. I was totally lost feeling like I was in way over my head.

I asked Bettie to give me a crash course in finances and to provide me with the most recent profit and loss statements. I hated feeling ignorant among the guys, but no matter how much I practiced, my financial acumen never matched the rest of the group.

However, I did know enough to know we were on target with our profit plan projections, when we could hire our next employee, what our payables were weekly and if any receivables were more than 30 days out. As far as my business was concerned, this was the information I needed to know to make decisions and understand our direction.

My lesson to anyone who struggles with the financial side of their business is this. Find the two or three key financial indicators that tell you when your business is running well. Get to know those indicators and track them consistently. Continue to add to your knowledge bank but don't try to match your financial knowledge to anyone else's. It's not about that. It's about knowing *your business*. And no one knows your business better than you!

I may not have been as knowledgeable as my peers in the financial side of a business, but I excelled at understanding how to engage employees and how to manage performance and productivity. When I focused on those aspects of our business, we were consistently profitable.

In the 14 years I helped manage that company, we only lost money in one year. It was the year we made a decision to focus on profit, not people. Lesson learned.

Have your CPA or accountant help you with the cash analysis process. However, abdicating the full responsibility and knowledge of this critical aspect of your business is a sure-fire way to fail. The more you understand how to best utilize *cash*, the more profitable and successful your company will be.

CASH FLOW MANAGEMENT ACTION STEPS

Sometimes, CEOs are in denial about the realities of cash flow. They can take a head in the sand approach, which predictably, leads nowhere fast.

Here are the top five rationalizations CEOs typically give to staff and vendors in cash flow crunches.

1. Things will get better tomorrow.
2. They said they would cut the check this week.
3. I am working on a big deal right now that will solve these problems.
4. I have to go to an important interview (which is a long shot, but more fun than thinking about cash).
5. Let me check with accounting and get right back to you.

To counteract this way of thinking, I have included the top five actions that CEOs in cash flow crunches should undertake to improve their chances of survival.

1. Examine cash flow and expense projections "realistically" for the next 90 days. Review the monthly deficit. Then, break the first month down into weeks. Do not leave the office on Friday without comparing actual to projected results. Adjust projections for week #2.
2. Dump any expenses not directly related to sales. Move administrative, accounting and marketing staff to part time, where possible. Reduce near term marketing expenses. Focus on business

development and lead generation from existing lines
of opportunity.

3. Network like crazy. Call old clients and keep your
face out in the community. Show confidence in
public, but be honest with yourself when analyzing
the numbers.

4. Get accounts receivable up to date. For anyone over
90 days, offer a discount for immediate payment.
Push for action for those at 61-90 days. Have lunch
with the CEO or your contact there. When a debt is
personal, people are more likely to take action. Don't
burn bridges.

5. Get bills out immediately. Micro-manage the bill
timing procedures for the near term. If you bill
monthly, do not wait until the end of the month to bill.

Review accounts receivable and accounts payable with your staff
at least twice weekly. Set fair but aggressive expectations.

Three important factors are directly **responsible for continual
cash flow challenges. Ask yourself:**

1. Am I paying attention or making excuses?
2. Is there a lack of managerial and financial
dashboards to gauge performance?
3. Do we have profit plans, or even quarterly plans in
place with goals and objectives listed?

TWO WAYS TO THINK ABOUT CASH

In Robert Fleury's excellent book, *The Small Business Survival Guide*, he clarifies how cash can be identified two ways: cold, hard green cash or goods and services that can be obtained and used without immediate payment of cash. The latter is considered the same as cash.

For example, many companies have operating cash because of bill payment deferral. Delayed payment for goods and services results in temporary free cash. For a better understanding of how this practice works, use the cash analysis form from page 184 of Fleury's book.

THE VALUE OF CASH MANAGEMENT AND ANALYSIS

To know your business is to know its financial strengths. Some feel the financial side isn't nearly as fun or sexy as the marketing and sales side. My mantra to business owners is this:

> If you aren't passionate about the financial aspects of your business you won't have a business to be passionate about.

You don't need to become a financial whiz kid. You just need to understand the metrics that tell you when things are working well and when things are going to _____ (you fill in the blank!).

Learning a little bit today will pay off in spades tomorrow. Check out my online program, Destination, Greatness: Your Financial

Success System (www.destination-greatness.com) for insights into building a financial foundation. This 12-module, self-directed program teaches you how to select key indicators, create a profit plan and other key fundamentals that help a business stay financially sound.

EXERCISE #3:

MAKE FINANCIAL LITERACY EVERYONE'S RESPONSIBILITY

In a program I offer on financial literacy (Zeroing in on Your Company's Profit Zone), I ask CEOs and their management teams ten questions from Perry J. Ludy's book, *Profit Building: Cutting Costs Without Cutting People.*

1. What are the top five most costly items on your company's profit and loss sheet?
2. What written action plans are in place to reduce cost for these five line items?
3. What are the company's variable costs and what have you done to reduce them?
4. What are the company's fixed costs and what have you done to reduce them?
5. Name five vendors from whom you purchase supplies or services. When was the last time you negotiated a better price from these vendors?
6. Which of your costs are down from a year ago and why?
7. What have you done to reduce labor costs in your area of responsibility?

8. What are you doing this week to reduce costs?
9. How do you know you are being charged the correct rate on your cell phone bills and your long-distance bills?
10. What amount of cost reduction is planned for next month?

Interestingly, not many managers can answer these questions. In fact, our discussion is often the first time these questions have come up. My experience in delivering this program has been positive. People want to know the answers to these ten questions. But the real goal is to start a conversation about profit and loss statements and profit planning in a way that is meaningful and engaging.

In my experience, business owners believe these financial myths:

- Employees have little interest in how their company makes money.
- Profitability can't be taught to employees who don't understand a financial statement.
- If employees knew how much money a company made, they would demand more money.

None of these myths are real but we all know that perception is reality. These myths prevent business owners from educating their employees about how the company makes and keeps money.

It makes little sense when the financial knowledge of a business is not widely shared, especially because the generation of revenue and profit occurs throughout an organization. Why should the financial operations be kept from the very people whose job it is to keep the company financially sound?

Better cash management starts with understanding how cash is generated, protected and saved. Take the time to educate your employees on the realities of running a business. Start small. Don't overwhelm them. Break the information down to where it's meaningful for the people doing the work. Your time investment will come back to you tenfold.

You don't have to share every nitty gritty detail of the finances with your employees to help them better understand how it all works. Simply open a dialogue about process efficiencies, or how easy or difficult it is to get payments out to vendors, or why that big contract you just landed doesn't mean you can afford to buy new computers for everyone. By talking about the business of business, you'll help your employees see things differently.

> Why should the financial operations be kept from the very people whose job it is to keep the company financially sound?

If the concept of "open book management," made popular by Jack Stack in his book, *The Great Game of Business*, has you clenching your teeth right now, stop. I am promoting straightforward education over a big reveal. Help your employees understand how they impact the big picture, so that their energy goes to contributing to it.

THE VALUE OF MAKING FINANCIAL LITERACY EVERYONE'S RESPONSIBILITY

If you buy into the three myths that I talked about, I encourage you to read *The Great Game of Business* to learn how powerful it can be when employees really understand how a company makes and keeps money.

As the Chief Operations Officer of that marketing communications company, I remember explaining billable hours to one of our graphic artists. His hours were consistently above and beyond what we had proposed for projects. I was taken aback when he explained that he felt it was his responsibility to deliver more than the client asked for and therefore didn't feel he needed to pay attention to the hours assigned for a project. I later understood that we had sent him mixed messages. We certainly wanted to provide our clients with the best work possible, but we also wanted people to stay within the number of hours we had proposed for projects. No wonder people were confused.

After that, I spent hours in conversations with all of our employees explaining what a billable hour was (they were, in essence, our product – we sold time). If we were given 40 hours of time in which to complete a project, going over meant we lost money. We had to encourage people to be honest in capturing their hours so we could bid on other projects and know the number of hours we were bidding would be enough to complete the job.

It took us months to help people understand overhead, projected hours versus actual hours and set up a system to track and record those hours. Financial literacy is what kept us from going bankrupt when the dotcom implosion occurred in March 2000. Because of the work we had done prior to that difficult period, that education on how we made and kept money paid off. When things got tight and we had to lay off 30% of our employees, people understood the issue. Everyone pulled together to help the company get to break even within three months and to show a profit in six.

RESOLVING THE CHALLENGE OF CASH FLOW

Remember the Flood Zone? It's the transition period between Stages 1 and 2 that causes many business owners to feel like they are drowning. The increase in activity (more issues, questions, challenges, employees, clients) also requires better bookkeeping, tracking of information and a more aggressive understanding of cash flow management.

As you ramp up for growth, your payroll expands. Without a profit plan (budget) and up-to-date financials, your company can spin quickly out of control.

Although the company is still CEO-centric, you are starting to delegate more and more authority and responsibility. Simultaneously, you need to educate your employees on how what they do every day impacts the bottom line.

It's my belief and experience that:

- If employees understand the value they bring to a company, they will be more engaged.
- If an employee is engaged, they will be more productive.
- A company full of productive employees will make more money.

Challenge #4: Leadership/Staff Communication Gap

This challenge creeps up on you overnight. As a Stage 1 company, with 1 – 10 employees, it's very easy to communicate often and effectively with your employees. In fact, people often refer to their companies in this growth stage as a family.

When my marketing communications company was in its early stages of growth, we gave out bonuses in the form of shopping trips and nights out on the town. We had an all female staff at the time, so shopping, seeing a play and having a great dinner fit all of us to a T! We really were one big happy family.

As we grew and added more employees, the gap between what leadership said and what employees heard widened. It became harder to maintain consistency in how employees were treated, it became harder to have all the answers and it became harder to keep everyone engaged.

And with up to 19 people to manage, that family atmosphere started to create its own set of issues. For instance, the employees who had started with us now felt threatened to some degree by the new people joining us. Why? Because those early Stage 1 employees were hired for fit not for specific skills.

As your company grows and starts to delineate specific tasks, you need to start hiring for specialized skill sets. If those employees who joined you early aren't encouraged to keep up their own skill development, the company will outgrow them. It's easy for the CEO to ignore this critical shift and simply assume those dedicated and loyal early stage employees will continue to hold their own.

Changes must be made and those changes push a business owner into areas they aren't necessarily comfortable dealing with. Such as:

- "Difficult" conversations.
- "Lack of performance" conversations.
- "You need to move on" conversations.

If leadership pulls back from these conversations, the communication gap becomes one of those obstacles that can hinder growth. There are two elements at odds here. The demands placed on a leader with a growing number of people to manage increases ten-fold and, according to a Gallup Study, 70% of American workers are either not engaged or are actively disengaged.

As we grew, we could no longer rely on the historical data banks of our trusted employees. It was essential that those processes were captured into manuals and onto systems. It became necessary to create performance plans to be able to reward employees with pay increases. The days of dropping $500 on a dinner as an incentive were over.

Out of necessity, systems begin to replace hands-on work that requires a lot of interaction. There is less opportunity for people to connect face-to-face, which only serves to widen the gap between leadership and staff. A Stage 2 leader must take proactive steps to break down the barriers. The sooner you can minimize this reality, the more successful your company will be.

> **70% of American workers are either not engaged or are actively disengaged.**

How does a leadership/staff communication gap impact your company?

- Low productivity
- Reduced efficiencies
- Increased rework
- High incidents of gossip
- Lack of commitment
- Customer service mistakes
- Project scope creep
- High turnover
- Finger pointing
- Blame placing

These are all huge problems that can take a company down. For this reason, dealing with the leadership/employee gap in Stage 2 isn't an option; it's a requirement.

People don't just become good managers, which is why this challenge is one of the hardest to eliminate. Good managers are taught; but when you are growing quickly, stopping to train people on how to be good managers doesn't usually make the prime time.

My belief is that your people are your business. Therefore, tending and nurturing them is what good management is all about. As the CEO of a Stage 2 company, you need to become good at managing people so that you can teach others to follow your lead.

Depending on your cash flow, you may even want to consider hiring a trained and experienced second-in-command to help you manage. Understandably, that may not be feasible at this time, but regardless, you have to set the stage for how your employees will engage and how your managers will lead.

> **Your people are your business.**

EXERCISE #1:

THE ONE-ON-ONE

This exercise will, without a doubt, solve 90% of your leadership/staff communication gaps. I actually guarantee it. It's called the one-on-one.

As a manager, you need to spend 30 minutes a week with each of your direct reports. The goal behind these meetings is to open up a dialogue. Notice I said dialogue, not a discussion about projects, or what work is being done or not being done. This meeting is about a manager connecting to an employee and an employee connecting to a manager on a level that creates a dialogue.

This process will break down the barriers every time. Why? Because it's an opportunity for a manager to appear more human and it's an opportunity for an employee to express their value.

MISSION:

The one-on-one meeting's mission is to establish responsibility, accountability and proactive behavior throughout the company. It also:

- Delivers and carries vital messaging between the manager and the employee that allows for clarity and truth.
- Demonstrates the importance that the employee's job/career development has to the enterprise's welfare.
- Becomes the vehicle that facilitates the individual to self-correct unproductive and unsupportive behavior.
- Builds the personal commitment to high performance at a DNA level in every employee.
- Trains for leadership succession.
- Is, ultimately, the primary cornerstone the organization has in place that makes the continued execution of its goals, strategies and plans a reality.

If meeting with employees on a regular basis has not been a part of a manager's thinking, start with small steps to establish this process as a welcome and engaging interaction.

STEP ONE: COMMIT THE TIME

Managing people takes time and as a CEO you have very little of this commodity. The first step in establishing a pattern of meetings with your employees is to select a fixed day and time and schedule the meetings six months in advance.

Commit to putting dates on your calendar and don't allow other pressing issues to derail the meeting. If for some reason you need to cancel the appointment, be sure to reschedule immediately so the process does not break down.

STEP TWO: THE FIRST MEETING

You've set the date and the employee will be showing up any minute. The first meeting has no agenda. This concept is as new to the employee as it is to you, so make it a relaxed but open meeting. Here are some suggested topics:

- Introduce the employee to the concept of the one-on-one. Let them know you are new to this but you are committed to providing an opportunity for productive dialogue every week or every two weeks, whatever your time frame is. (Once a week is ideal, every two weeks is okay. Once a month is not an option.)
- Explain the objectives of the one-on-one. Take them from this book and use your own words or give the employee a handout with the objectives.
- Explain the time commitment. The first couple of meetings may take up to 45 minutes, but as you get more used to the agenda and the flow, they can be done in 30 minutes. (If you want them to be an hour, that's fine. The point is to make them easy to handle

and of solid quality so you and the employee both get value.]

- Introduce key indicators for their area of responsibility. If you are talking with a project manager, ask them to come up with three key indicators they track on a regular basis that indicates the strength of their job performance.

- Explain that you are very interested in knowing how they define success for their area of responsibility. How they are performing in those key areas will give you a solid idea of their progress.

- Explain there may be other agenda items that either you or they bring to each meeting but the time commitment needs to be respected for both of you.

- Review when the next meeting is and make sure you both have it on your calendars.

Caution: These meetings are strictly about engaging the employee in meaningful dialogue about their progress. Be very clear that the employee can meet with you at other times to discuss difficult problems in more depth. If you allow your 30-minute, one-on-ones to become a two-hour long "how do we solve the project management issue on XYZ property," discussion, then you've lost the purpose behind the meeting. You won't be apt to hold them again because they took too much time. The one-on-ones are intended to open communication between you and your employee; they need to be protected for that purpose.

STEP 3: AFTER THE MEETING

Keep track of the things you talked about and the updates the employee gave you. How was their attitude? The interaction overall? Were they prepared? Were they confident and comfortable? Note follow up areas for next time. Maximum time spent on this piece: 5 minutes. Don't write a book.

SAMPLE AGENDA:

1. Welcome – a greeting or small talk to relax them.
2. Overview of your world – share with them a challenge you have had recently, a decision you made, a client you met with – something to open up and let them inside the world of a manager.

Adjust these suggested questions to fit your culture and your environment.

- What is working for you? What isn't working?
- Where do you need help?
- What do you suggest?
- What did you do last week that you are proud of?
- What did you learn over the past week?
- What do you need to learn?
- How will you learn it?
- What did you accomplish over the past week?
- What will you accomplish going forward?
- How will you accomplish it?

And always, no matter what questions you decide to ask, the last one is simply: How can I help? The employee will likely be reluctant to open up at fist, but patience and persistence is the name of the game.

THE VALUE OF THE ONE-ON-ONE

These questions are designed to draw out how the employee is *feeling* about their job, their career, their goals and their dreams. Most managers are only comfortable asking job or project related questions; these questions push buttons and gets them to dig deep, and ultimately, the relationship will deepen too.

> Patience and persistence is the name of the game.

The intention of the one-on-one is to enhance the quality of communication between managers and employees. Once the employee understands how they add value to the company, performance and engagement improves.

EXERCISE #2:

ENSURE EMPLOYEE ENGAGEMENT

No business owner wants to feel like they are babysitting his employees. Those horrible closed-door meetings about behavior can be avoided. If you're thinking of shrinking your company back to 5 – 6 employees because the thought of more employees gives you nightmares, you aren't alone. However, if you plan on growing your business and ramping up, employees are a part of that equation.

Engagement starts with trust. It evolves into respect. And in time, the ability to improve the engagement level in your company leads to a better bottom line.

As a business owner, you have a lot riding on how your business performs. I know I felt that pressure when I was running a company with 100 employees. It sometimes seemed that every single employee simply came to work, grabbed their paycheck and asked for time off.

I believe that when people communicate, problems are solved, trust is maintained, no one feels taken advantage of, egos get stroked and ideas get generated. I witness good employees struggling to succeed. I witness good managers struggling to understand their employees. I witness the heartache when a good employee has no other option but to leave and I witness the stress when a good manager throws up her hands in frustration over an employee who won't listen. I also witness bad employees staying too long and bad managers creating a negative work environment that can erode any success a business has obtained.

> **Engagement starts with trust.**

So, if you manage employees, listen up. Employees are human beings who have some basic needs. When those needs go unattended, the good ones leave and the bad ones stay. Both situations can take a good company down.

Jack, the owner of a small construction company for four years, recently received a phone call from Bill, his supplier. During the conversation, Bill mentioned a conversation he'd had with Jack's employee out in the field, in front of the owner of the project. Jack hung up from that call, walked into his employee's office and proceeded to rail on the employee about having *that kind* of conversation in front of an owner.

Jack didn't stop and ask for the employee's side of the conversation. He didn't call the owner to see if there was an issue or stop and ask if what Bill had said was true. He didn't think about the 25 years of experience his employee had, nor did Jack stop and think about the countless hours this employee puts in for him every week. Jack didn't stop and think about the best way to bring up this issue. He simply reacted and he reacted badly.

In fact, Bill had misled Jack. The context of the conversation wasn't out of line and the employee handled it with diplomacy. There was no issue with the owner of the project. But now there is an issue that Jack will be dealing with for a long time. Broken trust. And broken trust creates employee disengagement.

By simply taking the time to explore the situation and have a conversation with his employee, this very emotional situation could have had a much better outcome. That experienced, loyal employee is now questioning why he should stay. Over time, if this situation is left to fester, that employee will become one of the 70% actively disengaged employees.

Here are three steps you can take today to improve employee engagement at your company.

1. **Become a better leader.** According to John Maxwell's **The 21 Irrefutable Laws of Leadership,** "Leadership ability determines a person's level of effectiveness. The lower an individual's ability to lead, the lower the lid on her potential." In the example above, Jack's leadership

lid is low and he eventually lost that loyal and experienced employee because he refused to address his own limitations. If you want your company to get better, you need to be better. In Stage 2, the ability of the leader to paint the picture of what the company stands for and where the company is heading requires 40% of a leader's focus. The company is still CEO-centric and those 11 - 19 employees, who are working long days and many weekends, need to believe in the dream. They need to be able to see how their job, what they do every day, brings value to the company. What are you doing every day to provide encouragement to your staff? What are you doing every day to provide the leadership your staff needs to stay focused and engaged?

2. Learn how to have crucial conversations.
No one likes conflict, but as human beings conflict is in our nature. People have opinions, different values and different perspectives. So we aren't all going to get along every day. Bottled up tensions increase distance between two people. "I know what I said irritated John, but if I simply ignore it, he'll get over it." This type of internal conversation goes on in our employees every day. Your job is to make sure people feel comfortable having those tough conversations. Teach your employees that confrontation doesn't have to be an argument. Show them how to disagree with respect. Be the role model and encourage different opinions to show

up in staff meetings, team meetings and company meetings. Encourage people to say what's on their mind and to think in terms of solutions, not just problems. Those are intentional steps a leader can take every day to help employees embrace a culture of engagement.

3. **Be authentic.** You don't have to have all the answers all the time. When you aren't sure of something, admit it. Ask for advice. Set up situations where your employees can talk to you directly in relaxed settings. Join in lunchroom conversations. Invite people into your office and find out what they think about specific issues. Allowing people to see who you really are isn't a sign of weakness; it's a sign of strength and confidence. Find reasons to provide encouragement every time you have the opportunity. Your staff feels growth pains with increased workload, unfamiliar processes, dealing with different personalities and staying focused on providing great customer service. Look for opportunities where you witness exceptional work and make it a point to say thanks individually and share successes in front of the entire team. When people see that you willingly look for opportunities to uncover positive progress, they will do the same. You'll help your team weather that Flood Zone we talked about earlier.

By starting with these three small steps, your employees will see you making the effort to be a better leader, to address crucial conversations in a positive, respectful way and see you as someone who isn't afraid to admit when they don't know something and being able to ask for help.

THE VALUE OF ENSURING EMPLOYEE ENGAGEMENT

I work with companies all the time who struggle with this very difficult issue. In many cases, not only are the employees disengaged, the business owner feels held hostage by them. In some industries, just finding qualified people can be a challenge, so if an employee's performance is less than stellar, the business owner is hesitant to address it for fear the employee will leave and they won't be able to find someone else to fill the spot. Now we have a negative chain reaction of events. Bad performance is ignored, other people see the lack of accountability and become resentful and soon the entire company is mired in a morale issue that is extremely difficult to resolve.

Never has the need for a strong and capable leader been greater. Don't let one bad apple poison the barrel. Employee engagement begins with you and trickles down to your direct reports. If your direct reports see you model the three steps outlined above, they'll follow your lead. With your encouragement, they'll continue to create a culture that helps people see the value they bring to the company.

EXERCISE #3:

THE PERFORMANCE APPRAISAL SYSTEM

Nothing creates more tension between a manager and an employee than the dreaded performance appraisal meeting. If you've ever managed employees, you know the drill.

It's during this meeting that most salary discussions occur and it's often when employees hear a litany of their shortcomings for the first time, some of which may have occurred months prior, leaving those employees frustrated and defensive. Unprepared managers try to find positive things to say to decrease the impact of the negative. It never works. All an employee hears when they walk away from those unproductive meetings is everything they ever did wrong. The positive is lost somewhere in their resentment, embarrassment and anger. There are so many things wrong with the typical performance appraisal system that I could have written an entire chapter on it. This one seemingly necessary system single-handedly increases the leadership/staff communication gap in thousands of companies.

Instead, I'm going to give you some alternatives to this concept. I urge you to explore new and interesting performance management theories that make so much more sense than the traditional approach. I'll start with the traditional and blend in some of the ideas I've become familiar with then challenge you to start thinking about this system differently.

What is performance appraisal? The definition is a formal management system that evaluates the quality of an individual's performance in an organization. Often performance appraisal meetings are seen as a once-a-year event mandated by human resources. Or, in the case of smaller companies, by leaders or managers who remember their experience of performance appraisal systems and simply reintroduce something they are familiar with.

I'll break this down into FIVE steps. And remember, your performance appraisal system should be unique to your company and support your culture. Don't allow the complexity of performance appraisal systems to deter you from making this a critical part of your employees' expectations. These meetings are paramount to your company's success.

STEP ONE:
PAINT THE BIGGER PICTURE

Because we are talking about this process as a Stage 2 company, the approach is unique to your size today. As you grow, so must your processes.

As the CEO, it's your responsibility to set the goals for the organization. Your ability to define where the company is today and where you want it to be in 12 months determines how you will handle the performance planning sessions with your employees. Don't have this conversation in a vacuum. If you are on a calendar year, start early in October, and three months ahead if you are on a fiscal planning year.

Bring your employees together and help them understand the fundamentals of your business. Start small and make it meaningful to them.

TALK ABOUT:

- What your company stands for and the company's core values.
- Who your customers are and why they come to you.

- What your strengths are as an organization.
- What the company needs to do in order to make money.
- Explain what profit is and show examples of simplified financial statements.
- Help your employees connect the dots in terms of what they do every day and how they impact the bottom line.

How you evaluate your employees' performance has to start with where the company is going and how it's going to get there. Then, each employee needs to understand how what they do every day impacts those goals.

STEP TWO:
SET EXPECTATIONS AND
PERFORMANCE GOALS

Start by identifying the critical indicators for your company. A critical indicator is a metric that tells you two things: when things are going well and when they aren't.

For instance, if you are a service-based company, critical indicators may be billable hours or utilization, the break-even rate, number of leads generated, revenue per employee, dollar value of proposals sent out, dollar value of contracts closed and work in progress. You may keep it simple and identify monthly revenue goals, monthly gross profit goals or net profit targets every month. If you are in manufacturing, you may look at sales goals, manufacturing costs, on-time delivery, cycle time, efficiency issues like throughput or overall equipment effectiveness, inventory turn rates, customer rejects or returns.

It's your responsibility to engage your employees in a conversation that helps them see how each person's job impacts those key indicators. Once employees understand their key indicators and how they impact the company's overall indicators, you have a place to start regarding performance reviews. Now the conversation becomes: How are you performing against your key indicators this month?

Special Note: By Stage 2 you should already have systems inside your company set up to generate reports and track critical information. Consider QuickBooks for financial tracking, Pipeline Deals for sales tracking or Salesforce for customer relationship management. These are simply suggestions for a starting point.

STEP THREE: DETERMINE SALARY GOALS

As a Stage 2 company, you probably haven't put salary bands in place or clearly identified how an individual will earn more money. In the early stage of growth, salary raises are usually based on how well the company is doing financially, not how well the employee is performing. To begin the switch from what can quickly become a culture of entitlement (I deserve more money because of how many hours I put in) to a culture of responsibility (when I meet my performance goals, I'll see a 10% increase), you have to start educating your employees on what financial responsibility looks like.

Financial literacy should be a requirement of any employee that joins a company. If an employee feels they need to make more money but has no idea what they need to do in order for that to happen, the fault lies with the CEO, not the employee.

By using a profit plan (budget) to project your incoming revenues each month, your cost of goods and your general and overhead expenses, you'll be able to plan for salary increases. If you are running an annual payroll of $500,000 and expect to pay out salary increases on average of 15%, you'll need to budget an additional $6,200 a month to cover those increases.

How will you adjust your revenue goals in order to afford those increases? Explain to your employees that salary increases are tied to the company's ability to generate more revenue. You are starting down that financial literacy path and educating your employees on the realities of running a business.

STEP FOUR:
MONTHLY PERFORMANCE SESSIONS DRIVEN BY EMPLOYEES

Set the expectation that it's your employees' responsibility to report to you monthly how they are doing with their key indicators. Work with them to create a reporting structure that is consistent and easy to maintain. The goal is to drive your employees toward being responsible for their own performance updates. Train employees to provide a summary report on any key indicators that are not in line with goals and have them offer ideas and suggestions on how to improve for the next month.

Your role in these monthly meetings is to continually adjust employee's expectations regarding performance. Help them see the strengths that support their personal growth and their impact on the company's overall goals. If the employees' expectation is a salary increase of a certain percent if certain goals were met or exceeded, there will be no surprises during the annual performance review. The point is, this is not an annual conversation; it's an ongoing dialogue throughout the year.

STEP FIVE: THE ANNUAL PERFORMANCE CONVERSATION

In Exercise #1, you learned the process and the value of the one-on-one. With this process and the employee-driven monthly meetings in place, the annual performance review should be simply a review of how well the employee did overall and what salary increase they can expect based on their performance.

THE VALUE OF THE PERFORMANCE APPRAISAL SYSTEM

If you have up to 19 employees, you have started to delineate levels of responsibility in your company. Some of the weekly and monthly conversations may not involve you, as others may have taken on management responsibilities. Your role is to stay in touch with those supervisors and have them report to you how well their teams are doing. Starting an on-going performance review mindset in this early stage of your company's growth will serve you exceptionally well as you move into Stage 3 with up to 34 employees.

RESOLVING THE CHALLENGE OF LEADERSHIP/STAFF COMMUNICATION GAP

Here's what I will say about my own development as a leader. It happened painfully. I made many mistakes. As a supervisor of one of the first and largest recreation centers in Colorado, I was very naïve. I had just graduated from college and my approach with people was I:

1. Treated them all the same. After all, I wanted them all to do the same thing.
2. Acted like I knew everything because to do otherwise would be akin to showing how little I really knew.
3. If someone didn't respond to something I said, I would get defensive and tell them they were wrong.
4. Tried to get people to like me because if they liked me, they'd do what I asked.
5. Ignored gossip – there's no way to really know where or how gossip starts and no one really listens to it anyway.

Leadership skills don't magically appear with time. Upon going back to school and receiving my MBA, my approach to leadership changed overnight, thanks to a class that addressed the art and science of being a good leader. I continued to evolve and grow every day.

Volumes have been written on leadership. I found an article written by Ben Parr in 2010 that said Google used advanced algorithms to come up with this enticing and little known statistic:

There have been 129,864,880 books published in all of modern history! Google defined a book as a "tome" – an idealized bound volume. If even 5% of these are on leadership that means there are over 6,000,000 books on the topic! Why then, is leadership in such short supply?

The answer is because, ultimately, no one can become a better leader unless they want to.

Sure, go ahead and read all those books by well-known authors and impress your friends and business acquaintances with the number of books on your bookshelf. However, until you personally want to improve your leadership skills, all those books you bought are a waste of money.

I love books. I love reading all kind of books: fiction and non-fiction. And I confess, I don't read all business books cover to cover. I simply don't have the time. I do however, look over the Table of Contents, find a topic I want to know more about and flip over to that chapter. Then, I'm a maniac underlining, highlighting, making comments in the margins (this is why I always buy business books in hard or soft cover, never electronically). I'll even put notations about clients that I work with next to a particular statement and find a way to share that tidbit with them.

I read to learn and apply. And for me, that requires taking in manageable amounts of data that are meaningful right then. There is an amazing amount of knowledge out there in those 130,000,000 and growing collection of books. As a CEO of a growing organization, you have an obligation to grow ahead of your company or your company will only grow to your present level of expertise.

Find books and authors that you enjoy learning from. Improve your own leadership skills so you can continue to help your employees become better leaders.

My go-to-leadership expert is John C. Maxwell. I've personally met Mr. Maxwell and found him to be as authentic as they come. In fact, I have been through his leadership certification program. He walks his talk and is totally committed to helping people become better leaders.

If you haven't found a favorite of your own yet, I highly recommend you pick up his book, *The 21 Irrefutable Laws of Leadership,* and start there. I wish that someone had told me about that book when I was in the early stage of my career as a leader and a manager. Unfortunately, for me and the hundreds of employees I mentored and coached over the years, I only learned of Mr. Maxwell a short time ago. Funny. Here's someone who has written over 70 books on leadership and I never paid attention.

> You have an obligation to grow ahead of your company.

Several months ago, I received an endorsement on LinkedIn from Wayde, someone I had hired for a position in our marketing communications company and hadn't heard from in 13 years. I was surprised and delighted, so I quickly sent him an email back thanking him for reaching out and for the endorsement. I said it was so good to hear from him! Two days later I received this reply, "You know I think the world of you. You taught me what a leader should be and how a leader should act. Thank you for your example in my life."

That short, but impactful note helped me to realize that I had grown as a leader. I think that the greatest compliment a leader can receive is to know they've made a difference in someone's life. Remember Maxwell's Law of the Lid: your leadership ability determines your level of effectiveness. Increase your leadership skills and your company will respond in subtle and meaningful ways.

Challenge #5: Limited Capital to Grow

In Stage 2, your need for capital has increased. As the need for funds grows, you will be required to access an increasingly sophisticated investor seeking maximum return for assuming the risk of a new venture.

If you are interested in exploring the intricacies of financing a business, I recommend *Techniques of Financial Analysis: A Guide to Value Creation* by Erich Helfert. In this widely published and popular book, Helfert talks about the role decision making has in running a successful business. He created an in-depth view of how the financial side of a business operates, and says, "Experience has shown again and again that just as important as the choice of tools themselves (referring to the tools you need to analyze business operations), is the need to first develop a proper perspective by carefully framing the problem or issue."

As a Stage 2 owner, the ability to frame the problem starts, in my experience, with where you want the company to be at a specific time frame. Not just in terms of reaching specific indicator targets, such as the number of clients/customers, revenues or profits, but in the long view that takes your company beyond your immediate vision. For instance, if you are working with a product that is time sensitive to the market, a lack of capital will hinder you from day one. When business owners are product-focused, they tend to think longer view. If a business owner is in the service industry, the view is less well thought out. I mention this because limited capital to grow is a Stage 2 issue regardless if you deliver a product or a service.

Many business owners have the false mentality of, "If I just work hard, I'll succeed." Be smart and evaluate the amount of money your company will need to get off to a solid start. Having limited capital to grow can negatively impact your growth all along the way.

You should think about funding before you even consider starting a business. However, a company may get started quickly with organic growth and funding capital may not seem necessary in the first several years. But you may find the need to open up new markets, innovate new products or service offerings or open up new locations across the country. Any one of these avenues may force you into thinking about long-term capital expansion. Suddenly the need to tap into outside funding sources may look like your biggest challenge yet.

If you are a profitable business, with a sound client base, good management structure and low debt to equity ratios, you could land a bank loan. You can also get the attention of venture capitalists. There are lots of workshops and free websites that can show you the route to take if want to get VC money. However, be aware that historically, according to the Kauffman Foundation, less than 1% of U.S. companies have raised capital from VCs.

Regardless of how you get your capital, it's important that you figure out in advance how that money will be spent. Put together a solid profit plan and use it to hold your feet to the fire in terms of seeing a return on that investment every month. Don't allow your longer-term capital to get crossed up with your day-to-day operating capital.

EXERCISE #1:

IDENTIFY YOUR STARTUP FUNDING OUTLETS

The SBA, the Kauffman Foundation and your local banker will attest that the number one reason new business fail is because they lack capital. And for women entrepreneurs, it's even more challenging. According to research by The Clayman Institute for Gender Research at Stanford University, women lack connections within the "old boys network" of funding sources. The research also shows that professional investors have less confidence in women than they do in men to penetrate their intended markets. Internet sites such as WomanOwned.com provide insights about fundraising, business management and networking assistance to more than 3.5 million women business owners around the world.

Acquiring outside funding for your business requires persistence, and in some cases, creativity. Jay Turo, founder of the advisory and investment banking firm, Growthink, advises entrepreneurs to "be irrational" and appeal to potential investors emotionally rather than intellectually.

Disclaimer: all businesses are different, and therefore the levels of capital and the pace the funds will be expended will always fluctuate. The goal here is to outline the best practices for businesses in Stage 2.

Here are a couple of tips that are vital to smart planning.

Tip #1: **It is always best to have capital resources in advance of when your business needs it.**

There are few worse things for a business than when you start to feel the pinch of cash flow. It makes all decisions tougher. This symptom shreds your attention level and restricts your businesses potential.

Tip #2: **Avoid depleting your personal financial resources before seeking financing.**

You may think it is wise to go as far as you can before taking on debt. But consider how you will look to a lender when they ask for a personal financial statement. They want to see available equity, cash and cash equivalents. Debt, when used wisely, is a business's best friend. A bank will likely want a personal guarantee and if there are limited assets and cash, it makes the transaction unlikely. Small business bank loans are based on a lender believing in you and your ability to carry out a plan that will provide repayment of the loan.

There are four major pathways to funding, other than self-funding through family and friends.

1. STANDARD BANK DEBT FINANCING

You will meet with one person during the courting process to secure a bank loan. Your friendly business development officers have a job and that is to fill their pipeline with opportunities. They are sincere in their interest to help your business, however they are not the decision makers.

Once an application and all of the appropriate documentation is provided, the bank turns the data over to a credit-underwriting specialist. Their job is to meticulously analyze your submittal and poke holes in it. They are sensitive to risk. A low credit score, a tax lien or inconsistent tax returns are big red flags. The other big red flags relate to bankruptcy filings and unfulfilled obligations (defaults) to other banks.

Here are some of the key criteria banks use to further their understanding of your business and the opportunity.

Surveying the Landscape:

- You, the current business and your payment history
- Purpose of the loan and the amount requested; relationship to any current debt
- Type of loan (equipment, lease, line of credit or general business loan)
- Sources of repayment

- Competition
- Covenants and controls the bank can impose

Elements of Good Underwriting:

- Your competency, character, management and leadership experience
- Business type and industry considerations (predictability, cyclical nature and current stability)
- The business and personal collateral: ratio to loan and risk, liquidity, ability to control your business, contingency risk. In the case of default, the bank's ability to establish possession.
- Remedies and ability to keep the business and ownership on track
- Risk and return consideration

Hiding or failing to report bad news on your application is very unlikely to go unnoticed. Banks share data. They have access to a depth of information on your personal credit. Don't waste time, it will only come up later and you will lose credibility.

To maximize the value of a bank loan for your business, talk with a few different banks and then ascertain which one you can imagine creating a good working relationship with. You can demonstrate your goodwill and receive their willingness to assist through pro-active communication.

2. SBA LOAN PROGRAMS

The SBA has a number of programs for different types of companies. Shown below is a summary of the different programs and their focus, percent of guaranty, benefit to borrowers and who is qualified. Download the chart at www.bizchallenges.com/referenceSBALoans.

QUICK REFERENCE TO SBA LOAN GUARANTY PROGRAMS — SBA U.S. Small Business Administration

Program	Maximum Loan Amount	Percent of Guaranty	Use of Proceeds	Maturity	Maximum Interest Rates	Guaranty Fees	Who Qualifies	Benefits to Borrowers
7(a) Loans	$5 million	85% guaranty for loans of $150,000 or less; 75% guaranty for loans greater than $150,000 (up to $3.75 million maximum guaranty)	Term Loan. Expansion/renovation; new construction, purchase land or buildings; purchase equipment, fixtures, lease-hold improvements; working capital; refinance debt for compelling reasons; seasonal line of credit, inventory or starting a business	Depends on ability to repay. Generally, working capital & machinery & equipment (not to exceed life of equipment) is 5-10 years; real estate is 25 years.	Loans less than 7 years: $0 - $25,000 Prime + 4.25% $25,001 - $50,000 P + 3.25% Over $50,000 Prime + 2.25%; Loans 7 years or longer: 0 - $25,000 Prime + 4.75% $25,001 - $50,000 P + 3.75% Over $50,000 Prime + 2.75%	(No SBA fees on loans of $150,000 or less approved in FY 2014.) Fee charged on guarantied portion of loan only. $150,001-$700,000 = 3.0%; $700,000 - $1,000,000 + 3.5%, plus 3.75% on guaranty portion over $1 million. Ongoing fee of 0.52% on loans over $150,000.	Must be a for-profit business & meet SBA size standards; show good character; credit, management, and ability to repay. Must be an eligible type of business. Prepayment penalty for loans with maturities of 15 years or more if prepaid during first 3 years. (5% year 1, 3% year 2 and 1% year 3)	Long-term financing; improved cash flow; Fixed maturity; No balloons; No prepayment penalty (under 15 years)
7(a) Small Loans Is any 7(a) loan $350,000 and under, except the Community Advantage and Express loans	$350,000	Same as 7(a)	Same as 7(a)	Same as 7(a)	Same as 7(a)	Same as 7(a)	Same as 7(a). Plus, all loan applications will be credit scored by SBA. If not an acceptable score, the loan can be submitted via full standard 7(a) or Express	Same as 7(a)
SBAExpress	$350,000	50%	May be used for revolving lines of credit (up to 7 year maturity) or for a term loan (same as 7(a)).	Up to 7 years for Revolving Lines of Credit including term out period. Otherwise, same as 7(a).	Loans $50,000 or less; prime+ 6.5% Loans over $50,000, prime + 4.5%	Same as 7(a)	Same as 7(a)	Fast turnaround; Streamlined process; Easy-to-use line of credit
SBA Veterans Advantage 01/01/14 - 09/30/14	Same as SBAExpress	Same as SBAExpress	Same as SBAExpress	Same as SBAExpress	Same as SBAExpress	No guaranty fee Ongoing fee of 0.52% on loans above $150,000.	Same as 7(a). Plus, small business must be owned and controlled (51%+) by one or more of the following groups: veteran, active-duty military in TAP, reservist or National Guard member or a spouse of any of these groups, or a widowed spouse of a service member or veteran who died during service, or a service-connected disability.	Same as SBAExpress; No guaranty fee
CapLines: 1. Working Capital; 2. Contract; 3. Seasonal; and 4. Builders	$5 million	Same as 7(a)	Finance seasonal and/or short-term working capital needs; cost to perform; construction costs; advances against existing receivables, consolidation of short-term debts. May be revolving	Up to 10 years, except Builder's CAPLine, which is 5 years	Same as 7(a)	Same as 7(a)	Same as 7(a). Plus, all lenders must execute Form 750 & 750B (short-term loans)	1. Working Capital - (LOC) Revolving Line of Credit 2. Contract- can finance all costs (excluding profit) 3. Seasonal - Seasonal working capital needs. 4. Builder - Finances direct costs when building a commercial or residential structure
Community Advantage Mission-focused lenders only Expires 03/15/17	$250,000	Same as 7(a)	Same as 7(a)	Same as 7(a)	Prime plus 6%	Same as 7(a)	Same as 7(a)	Same as 7(a) Plus lenders must be CDFIs, CDCs or micro-lenders targeting underserved market

U.S. Small Business Administration
10 S. Howard Street, Suite 6220
Baltimore, MD 21201

Baltimore District Office
(410) 962-6195
www.sba.gov/md

Information current as of March 2014
SBA Programs and services are provided on a nondiscriminatory basis.
See the SOP for the most up to date detailed information

3. CROWDFUNDING

Crowdfunding was created in the Jumpstart Our Business Startups Act of 2012 (JOBS). This new funding mechanism allows small companies with an annual income of less than $100,000 to raise up to $1 million through a simplified registration procedure with limited financial information.

Now a significant player in the world of small business enterprise funding, crowdfunding is used for a multitude of businesses and creative endeavors that otherwise would be left without a path to cash. The website, www.massolution.com, put out a report indicating that crowdfunding raised approximately 2.7 billion in 2012, and was expected to grow by almost double in 2013.

There are two main models for crowdfunders. The first is donation based funding. Donors contribute in respect to a collaborative goal, in return for products, perks or rewards. The second model is the investment approach.

Some Key Sites to Consider:

- Kickstarter: creative based, donation funding focused on the arts, film and video, dance, photography and journalism.
- Startup Crowdfunding: a global crowdfunding service to connect startups, crowd investors and business angels in over 150 countries. Used as a conduit to attract more serious business investors. They claim to have 100,000 profiles and 20,000 investors.
- Crowdfunder: solely an investment funding vehicle, Crowdfunder is a strong player in crowd investment funding. Generally funds mid to large amounts for businesses.
- RocketHub: offers a "success school" and best practices pathways to generate interest in your initiative. All types of products and businesses are listed. RocketHub is strategically aligned with A&E Project Startup, a group that searches RocketHub to bring your product to life.
- appbackr: focused on early seed, donation-based funding solely for mobile apps, using their campaign tool, Marketplace. A showcase for the very best apps.

It also provides an "appscore," a predictive analytical ranking system, scoring on intrinsic quality, user traction and sentiment.

- AngelList: established for tech startups with a significant lead investor in place. Predominantly Silicon Valley, geo-centric based opportunities. (Must also be incorporated in Delaware.)
- Quirky: a collaborative portal for donation-based crowdfunding if you are an inventor. Quirky offers a community to move the needle on progress.
- Peerbacker: donation funding for all types of projects; most are smaller scale in nature, but there are also a number of mid to larger scale. (A 5% success fee is charged for funds raised.)
- MicroVentures: a crowdfunded investment bank. They conduct detailed due diligence on startups and, if approved, they help raise capital from angel investors. They are a FINRA registered broker dealer. Main areas of interest are Internet technology, media and entertainment, software, green tech, mobile, social and gaming.

4. ANGEL FUNDING

Instead of going to an aggregator like MicroVentures, AngelList or Startup Crowdfunding, you can also seek capital the old-fashioned way and reach out to the Angel Club in your area.

Why are they called Angels? Because they are people who have earned their nest egg and are ready to give back. Angels enjoy the process of being engaged in something they have an interest in, or someone they see as investment worthy.

Generally, their primary motivation is to be engaged as a mentor throughout the startup process. John May, of New Vantage Group, wrote a book called, *Every Business Needs an Angel*. He does a great job of illuminating the motivations and value propositions the right Angel can bring to your business.

Angel participants may pool their resources on one company. Investors will want to see a local Angel or lead investor geographically near your business. Start to think locally.

Angels typically are the seed funding and early round funding source; they come in after your personal investment has occurred. Their investment range can be as low as $25,000 and as high as $800,000 (possibly even higher).

THE VALUE OF IDENTIFYING STARTUP FUNDING OUTLETS

There has never been a better time to be a borrower. Low interest rates, a large, active and well-prepared investment community and an improved economy succeeding in a weaker global system prove this. Remember, the U.S. entrepreneurship pool is likely the best-trained group ever.

In 1983, there were six schools dedicated to the pursuit of degrees in Entrepreneurship. Today, there are over three thousand. If you believe you could use some online education on starting your company, go to the FastTrac section at www.kauffman.org, which has provided training to more than 300,000 entrepreneurs.

Your job as a Stage 2 business leader is to have accurate personal financial statements, a passion for what you do and the time to pursue those investors most likely to be interested in your offering.

The Tools You Need to Raise Money:

- A one to two page summary stating the year founded, industry, product or service and location of the business.

- This document should also cover the funding strategy, management team, strategic advisors and other useful information.

- The main content should include the problem, your solution, target market, competitors, competitive advantage, marketing strategy and your revenue model.

- A detailed two-year sales and expense projections, footnoting key issues and assumptions made to the plan. It is essential for you to be honest about the threats to your plan. Having realistic numbers is well received compared to the "hockey-stick" look to sales and profits. Show months of slower cash intake and higher expenses. Sensitizing your numbers to the variables all businesses face enhances serious consideration.

- If you are presenting to Angels, you will need a concise 10-15 slide deck that covers the key points to tell your story. Many times the Angel will have a certain format they wish to be used.

- Last is an executive summary (four to six pages) to lead your investors in a narrative format to know more

about the opportunity, your value proposition and why
you and your team are going to be successful.

EXERCISE #2:

OTHER OPTIONS FOR FINDING CAPITAL

Become acquainted with your state's office of economic development and stay up to date with their website. Many states offer grants for small businesses to encourage economic growth. The advantage with a grant, of course, is it won't dilute the value of your company. They may be specific to an industry (such as technology) or purpose (international business development), so take the time and become familiar with opportunities available.

Because your company is growing, your options of getting outside funding have also expanded. Explore the myriad of grants and financing options many states offer to promote economic development.

In Colorado for instance, the Advanced Industries Accelerator Programs, under the direction of the office of economic development, promotes growth and sustainability in seven of Colorado's industries by helping to drive innovation, accelerate commercialization, encourage public-private partnerships and increase access to early stage capital.

The AZ Fast Grant program in Arizona offers early stage technology companies with training and technical assistance to commercialize their innovations, grow their business and create jobs.

The Arizona Commerce Authority offers the AIAF Program (Arizona Innovation Accelerator Fund) that provides debt financing to rapidly expanding Arizona businesses that need resources in order to capitalize on market opportunities. To be eligible for these programs, you must demonstrate your potential to create or retain employment opportunities for Arizonans. They tend to focus on companies with fewer than 500 employees.

Accion, serving Arizona, Colorado, Nevada, New Mexico and Texas is an award-winning 501(c) (3) nonprofit organization that increases access to business credit, makes loans and provides training. Seasonal loans as small as $500 - $8,000 are available for businesses that have been operating for six months or more. You can apply online, in person or over the phone for loans up to $1,000,000.

Prosper.com is an example of raising capital online and, according to their website, is "America's first peer-to-peer lending market-place." Borrowers list loan requests between $2,000 and $35,000 and individual lenders determine which loans to invest in. While the normal criteria still applies, such as having good credit, Prosper.com positions itself as an alternative to high-interest credit card debt and will respond to borrowing requests faster than a bank.

If you are looking to gain quick access to cash without obtaining a loan or selling major parts of your company, accounts receivable factoring is an option. Factoring companies purchase business receivables that are in good standing at a discount for cash. Purchase amounts are usually from 75 – 90% of the total value of the receivables and they usually require that the receivables are less than 90 days old.

Other resources committed to helping small businesses in most states include:

- SBDC – Small Business Development Council
- SBA – Small Business Administration
- Chambers of Commerce
- United States Department of Labor – Office of the Small and Disadvantaged Business Utilization
- National Federation of Independent Business

THE VALUE OF OTHER OPTIONS FOR CAPITAL

Knowledge is your best friend if you are a business owner in need of capital to grow. Talk to your banker. Talk to your local SBA or SBDC and leave no stone unturned in your search to fund your business.

Of course, a strong credit score, several years worth of tax returns, being in business for a couple of years and a formal business plan are standard requirements and you should be prepared to provide these as well as personal bank statements in order to qualify. But like everything that is worth having in life, it requires hard work and persistence. In doing research for this book, I was amazed to find so many options for raising capital. It is worth your time to be diligent in searching for that needed capital boost.

RESOLVING THE CHALLENGE OF HAVING LIMITED CAPITAL TO GROW

Your options for finding effective funding sources increased as you started having positive cash flow, sound receivables, a growing employee base and loyal customers.

Having limited capital to grow can negatively impact growth at all stages; not just in terms of reaching specific indicator targets (such as the number of clients, revenues and profits), but also in the long view that takes the company beyond its immediate vision. Working with a strategy and business planning professional will bring out the best at this critical stage and allow you to focus on day-to-day activities. The money spent on the front end will more than pay for itself in the long run.

The popular financial blog, *Money Crashers*, by Michael Lewis says, "The most egregious, indefensible mistake an entrepreneur can make when seeking capital is asking for too little to have a chance at success. When calculating the capital you need, plan that everything will take twice as long and cost twice as much as you expect. Figure that your worst-case scenario will occur, not your best case. Don't assume instant profitability, a common mistake of many first-time entrepreneurs, according to the National Federation of Business."

> Having limited capital to grow can negatively impact growth at all stages.

Here are some best practices for getting the funds you need.

1. Get your financial house in order. Check your credit scores and correct any issues before you apply.
2. Gather essential business records, including tax returns and financial statements. For an SBA loan you'll also need a formal business plan.
3. Define your goals specifically. Where are you going as a business? What will you do with the money? How much do you need? Ask for a specific amount that matches your strategy — not what you think you can borrow.
4. Be realistic, especially about your strengths and weaknesses. Loan officers will be evaluating your business thoroughly. Make sure you're upfront and proactive in communicating any challenges or opportunities for your business.

Understand your options and the process. For example, loan decisions below $100,000 may be made based on credit scores and basic information, while larger amounts will trigger a detailed review of your finances.

According to a Gallup study, venture capitalists invested $30 billion in startups in 2013, while 40% of VC-backed companies failed and 40% failed to provide a return. So while having enough capital is critical, the study went on to say that exceptionally talented entrepreneurs are the true indicator of a company's success. Money can't by itself grow your business. Only you, the business owner, can do that.

What's Next?

The great thing about understanding your challenges upfront is that you can work on them immediately and move on! You don't have to worry about where to devote your time and you have a clear outline of how to move your company from 11 - 19 employees to 20 - 34 employees. As a leader of a Stage 2 organization, you are at the beginning stages of navigating your own growth curve.

Business owners who have the ability to focus on the right things at the right time build successful businesses. If you make sure that you are working on these five challenges every day, your company will respond and reward you with results.

Many business owners are not able to put words to their issues. They simply know there are issues hitting them every day and they *react* to each issue separately, depending upon how critical the issue is at that exact day and hour. Reacting to issues is not an effective way to grow a business. Understanding your key issues, identifying them and working on them is a formula for success!

As a company grows, so must the leader. Each stage of growth will require something different. Understanding what is required of you as your company evolves can either propel the company forward or cause the company to stagnate: profits never materialize, sales suffer and there is high employee turnover.

> *"Understanding the 7 Stages of Growth has every single person, including myself, looking at the company differently. We are having different conversations. Employees have ownership of their departments. We talk about our obstacles to growth and how to address them monthly. Employees are now focused on where the company makes money and they are constantly looking at areas where we can improve profitability. People are stepping up and protecting our profit. They are totally engaged.*"
> – Kitty Evans, President, Evco Industries, Stage 1 Company.

Sales Ramp Up is the name of the game in a Stage 2 company. As you move closer to Stage 3 (20 – 34 employees) the priority shifts to delegating roles and responsibilities. Stage 3 is about learning how to "let it go to let it grow" in order to help the company become Enterprise-centric. The bottom line in understanding the 7 Stages of Growth is that the complexity of an organization will always extract its due.

Are you ready to tackle the Stage 3 Challenges? My book, *The Art of Delegation: Let It Go to Grow with 20 – 34 Employees,* offers tips on how to address the top five challenges for the third stage of growth.

> The complexity of an organization will
> always extract its due.

Take a look at our website, www.bizchallenges.com, for additional products and services for business owners who are passionate about turning their growing business into a great business.

FOUNDATION BUILDING BLOCKS FOR A STAGE 2 COMPANY WITH 11 – 19 EMPLOYEES

As a Stage 2 business in the Ramp-Up phase, you are probably experiencing a number of the following. If you are not, it may indicate that the company has not yet matured into a Stage 2 business.

AREA	DESCRIPTION
Employees	You have 11 to 19 employees. It's now more difficult for the CEO to make all the decisions. The people you hired in Stage 1 need your leadership direction to help them transition to more specific roles in Stage 2. Your ability as a leader has to increase in order for your company go grow.
CEO/Founder	You are the 'specialist' (sales/marketing or technical guru or inventor). Accurate self-assessment, having a deep understanding of your own emotions, as well as your own strengths and weaknesses is a competency worth building on in Stage 2.
Team	You have a team that is dedicated to the vision. But, staff members are looking for more autonomy, which is a challenge. You have to start delegating roles and responsibility to capable staff.

Business Model	You have found a successful business model but you continue to explore other market opportunities.
Climate	You and your staff are excited because the business is growing and is showing great promise. But, at the same time, the increase in activity is challenging the entire team. You go through the transition zone known as the Flood Zone where the level of activity is increasing daily and you and your team feel like they are drowning.
Systems	It's a critical time to start putting processes and systems in place. Identify key indicators and begin tracking critical information. It will be difficult because you are just getting around to identifying roles and responsibilities and people will be confused by the structure required for growth.
Cash	Cash continues to be a challenge with an expanding payroll, need for additional equipment and possibly more space. Increase sales volume, while necessary, offers specific challenges you can't ignore.
Focus	It is all about growing sales and putting in place processes that can be replicated.

A STAGE 2 COMPANY AT A GLANCE

CEO-CENTRIC

Number of Employees:	11-19
Number of Managers:	1
Number of Executives:	1
Builder/Protector Ratio:	3:1
Three Gates of Focus:	Profit/Revenue
	Process
	People
Three Faces of a Leader Blend:	Visionary 40%
	Manager 20%
	Specialist 40%
Leadership Styles:	Primary - Coaching
	Secondary - Pacesetting
	Auxiliary - Commanding
Leadership Competencies:	Emotional self awareness
	Accurate self assessment
	Inspirational
	Empathy
	Developing others
Critical Processes for Stage 2:	Financial
	Sales
	Production
	Human resources
	Work community
Critical Activities for Stage 2:	Profit plan is set up
	Defining roles and responsibilities
	Defining sales activity
	More emphasis on accountability

ARE YOU READY FOR STAGE 3 - DELEGATION?

There is no more difficult stage of growth to navigate then moving from Stage 2 with 11 – 19 employees to Stage 3 with 20 – 34 employees. The reasons are numerous, so if you are making this move, I encourage you to pick up my next book in this series: *The Art of Delegation: Let it Go to Grow with 20 – 34 Employees.*

As a CEO of at Stage 3 organization, you will be called upon to change how you think about your business, starting with the movement from CEO-centric to Enterprise-centric all the way to knowing what to delegate and what not to delegate.

Your top challenge in Stage 3 is Staff Buy-In and your top gate of focus is People. If you aren't ready to take on a much more visible management role, you'll need to find someone who can.

This stage of growth is where you move beyond having control over everything and begin helping key employees step up and take on more authority and responsibility. It's hard and requires patience and a strong Coaching leadership style, while still staying on top of critical issues. Your Builder/Protector Ratio is 1:1.

Stage 3 is where so many business owners begin to recognize what Fischer uncovered in his research that led to the concepts under-lying the 7 Stages of Growth. Complexity increases due to people. Becoming a better leader is not an option; it's a requirement.

The name of this stage of growth is Delegation. When you delegate, you empower someone else to act for you. That basic definition explains why delegation is problematic for so many small business owners. Delegation requires giving some control away.

Business owners tend to believe that no one else can do things as well as they can, but you cannot make every single decision and do all of the work single handedly! By better understanding the dynamics of being a Stage 3 leader, the transition can be accomplished successfully as long as you, the leader, are willing to "let it go to let it grow."

Visit us at www.bizchallenges.com to order Laurie's series of How To books based on the 7 Stages of Growth.

Survive and Thrive:
How to Unlock Profits in a Startup with 1-10 Employees.

Sales Ramp Up:
How to Kick Start Performance and Adapt to
Chaos with 11-19 Employees.

The Art of Delegation:
How to Effectively Let Go to Grow with 20-34 Employees.

ADDITIONAL RESOURCES

Adler, Lou: *Performance-based Hiring*

Bonnstetter/Bowers: *Talent/Unknown: 7 Ways to Discover Hidden Talent & Skills*

Bossidy, Larry and Charan, Ram: *Execution: The Art of Getting Things Done.*

Buckingham, Marcus and Coffman, Curt: *First Break All the Rules*

Dotlich, David and Cairo, Peter: *Why CEOs Fail*

Fischer, James: *Navigating the Growth Curve: 9 Fundamentals that Build a Profit-Driven, People-Centered, Growth-Smart Company*

Flamholtz, Eric G. and Randle, Yvonne: *Growing Pains*

Fleury, Robert: *The Small Business Survival Guide*

Goleman, Daniel; Boyatzis, Richard and McKee, Annie: *Primal Leadership: Realizing the Power of Emotional Intelligence*

Harnish, Verne: *Mastering the Rockefeller Habits*

Helfert, Erich: *Techniques of Financial Analysis: A Guide to Value Creation*

Ludy, Perry: *Profit Building: Cutting Costs Without Cutting Peopl*

Maxwell, John C.: *21 Irrefutable Laws of Leadership*

May, John: *Every Business Needs an Angel*

Pink, Daniel: *To Sell is Human*

Sinek, Simon: *Start with Why*

Slywotsky, Adrian: *The Profit Zone*

Stein, Mark; Christiansen, Lilth: *Successful Onboarding: A Strategy to Unlock Hidden Value within Your Organization*

Wheatley, Margaret J.: *Finding Our Way: Leadership for an Uncertain Time*

Zoble, Adrienne: *The Do-Able Marketing Plan*

HIRE LAURIE AS A SPEAKER!

Laurie Taylor has spoken to thousands of business audiences. Her topics include organizational growth, using the 7 Stages of Growth as a foundation, leadership development and employee engagement.

CRACKING THE CODE TO YOUR COMPANY'S GROWTH

Challenging insights into how companies grow based on a unique research study that shows the complexity level increases as you add people. Knowing your stage of growth provides predictability about growing a business that you can't find anywhere else.

YOUR PEOPLE ARE YOUR BUSINESS

The biggest challenge we face as business owners is the management of people. We all know people leave managers, not companies. If you address the reality of "your people are your business" early on in your company, managing profitability, performance and productivity will be easier. Learn how to break down barriers that exist between managers and employees and create relationships that engage and encourage employees to excel.

EVERYTHING RISES AND FALLS ON LEADERSHIP

Who are the leaders in your organization? Is leadership improvement an intentional part of your company's culture? John Maxwell, the voice of leadership and author of over 70 books on the subject, identified five levels of leadership – Position, Permission, Production, People Development and Pinnacle. Learn how to apply these principles and extend your own influence as a leader to build a culture of responsibility and authenticity.

You can reach Laurie at laurie@igniteyourbiz.com.

LAURIE'S CLIENT TESTIMONIALS:

"Before I tallied the evaluation forms, I knew that you were a hit! You were able to appeal to a group of business owners and top executives who are diverse in their industries, in their stage of business and in the sizes of their organizations. As I mentioned to you, this market has many one-person businesses, but I also have some of the largest employers in the region as members. You addressed the entire range with great success."

- Ken Keller, STAR Consulting

"Successful business owners will usually figure it out, but often only after it has become a problem. The Navigating the Growth Curve model is uncanny in its ability to accurately predict what is about to happen to business owners, so they can act before it costs them time, emotional energy and money.

As for Laurie Taylor, I gave her a real challenge: give a three-hour presentation to 35 business owners and senior executives. The real challenge? Our group represented every conceivable size and type of company from startups to Fortune 50, from law firms to manufacturing to technology companies. Laurie nailed the presentation giving tremendous value to everyone in the audience. After three hours, these top executives were still in their seats and taking notes. Now that is impressive!"

- Bill McIlwaine, Renaissance Executive Forums

"Laurie's presentation received rave reviews at our annual professional conference. Several attendees commented that she was the 'best value' in the entire conference, and 'worth the price of admission!'

Here are other comments we received. Great presentation!

Laurie was excellent. She was worth the price of the entire conference.

By far the BEST presentation at this conference. Laurie's dynamic, real, humble and confident.

Outstanding! I would take it again!

Stars! Worth the cost of coming here alone. Extraordinary.

The best value in the entire CMI conference.

Very motivating and engaging, as well as a good reminder of essentials.

Bring this one back next year."

- Susan Whitcomb, Career Masters Institute

"Laurie's program is credible because she has been through growing a business as a business owner. Her presentation offered succinct tips on how to focus on my business."

- Will Temby, Greater Colorado Springs
Chamber of Commerce

"Very informative and extremely eye opening! I really appreciated Laurie's honesty in talking about her own mistakes as a business owner."

- Jon Hicks, Hicks Benefit Group

"Laurie Taylor conducted a 4-hour workshop on the Stages of Growth for 30+ company CEOs, plus several of their management team. She effectively walked the entire group of companies to a clear understanding of this dynamic business model. In addition, she facilitated exercises that allowed the CEOs and their executives to begin to map out plans on how to manage their businesses. She had all parties engaged throughout the workshop.

Prior to being exposed to the Stages of Growth, some of the companies were like bumper cars bouncing around with limited forward motion, focusing on the non-important issues. The Stages are the GPS of business growth in that they provide clarity, focus and direction. Several companies that attended are now implementing the tools and processes that will lead to growth and improved profitability.

I recommend Laurie Taylor and the Stages of Growth to any business entity."

- Tony Hutti, Executive Forums

ACKNOWLEDGEMENTS

As I mentioned in my first book, *Survive and Thrive: How to Unlock Profits in a Startup with 1 – 10 Employees*, this series of books has been a vision of mine for years. I wrote it with the hope that, in a small way, it will help us to reverse the trend of so many small businesses failing within the first five years. Small business has been, and can be again, the economic engine we need to create jobs.

My thanks go out to the people I've worked with and who have been a part of my circle of friends and business associates. I appreciate their counsel, their friendship and their support.

Ralph Crozier, my business partner, for his guidance, his help with developing the content, his constant encouragement and his belief in me, which took an idea I'd had for three years and helped me turn it into a reality. www.strategyplus.net

Brooke White, my editor, whose skills and insight were invaluable in editing and pushing me to add critical pieces of information the reader will benefit from. I appreciate her patience and her experience. www.brookewhite1.com

Kim Hall, from Inhouse Design Studio, who created the front and back covers and layout for the book. Her creativity helped make the book come alive. www.inhousedesignstudio.com

James Fischer, for his research on the 7 Stages of Growth and his focus on the small business owner.

My clients over the years, who have taught me so much and allowed me to be their trusted advisor.

I'd also like to thank my Master Mind group. I so value their friendship and business insights. I could not ask for a better support group. Tom Dearth (www.tomdearth.com), John Marx (www.copsalive.com), Terri Norvell (www.furtherperformancegroup.com), Karyn Ruth White (www.karenruthwhite.com), Karen VanCleve (www.KarenVanCleve.com).

And most of all to my husband, Dave, who is always there to listen and to help and to remind me that I can do whatever I put my mind to. His support is the most meaningful because he is the one who puts up with my late nights and early morning writing binges where I barely acknowledge that night turned into day. He is always there with a hug and a word of encouragement and an invite to join him on our front porch for that very much appreciated glass of wine.

Made in the USA
Charleston, SC
03 February 2017